MISSILE!MISSILE!MISSILE!

A Personal Experience

By

Mike Brown

IN MEMORIAM

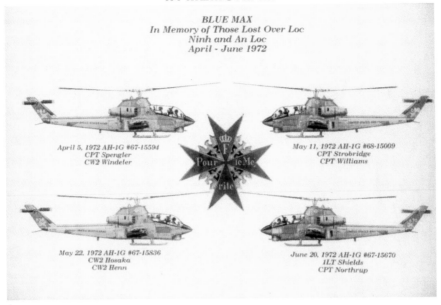

BLUE MAX
In Memory of Those Lost Over Loc
Ninh and An Loc
April - June 1972

April 5, 1972 AH-1G #67-15594
CPT Spengler
CW2 Windeler

May 11, 1972 AH-1G #68-15009
CPT Strobridge
CPT Williams

May 22, 1972 AH-1G #67-15836
CW2 Hosaka
CW2 Henn

June 20, 1972 AH-1G #67-15670
1LT Shields
CPT Northrup

The men whose names are inscribed above paid the ultimate sacrifice on behalf of their comrades and their countrymen during the Battles of Loc Ninh and An Loc during the period from April 5, 1972 to June 30, 1972. We pray that their sacrifice was not in vain. They are not forgotten.

(Artwork by Joe Kline; used by permission)

DEDICATED TO LAWRENCE (LARRY) E. McKAY
Lieutenant Colonel, U.S. Army, Retired

***The author, Mike Brown, and Larry McKay at Larry's home in Mt. Pleasant,
South Carolina in August 2011***

LTC Lawrence E. (Larry) McKay is mentioned frequently in this story. I cannot tell this story adequately or completely without a statement telling of Larry's great influence on my life. There are many others, whose lives have been touched by Larry, who would quickly express similar regard for him. Quite simply, Larry was the best boss with whom I've had the privilege of working. When he commanded F Battery, 79th Artillery (Blue Max) in Vietnam he didn't just command and lead. Larry loved his men. He demanded highly, but he "walked his talk." Men who served in Blue Max maintenance crews, to this day, express profound respect and love for the man who would show up after midnight in the early morning hours to express his appreciation for their work and their sacrifices. During those dismal days when pilot losses at the Battle of An Loc seemed so desperate, no one in the unit felt the pain of loss more than Larry. Larry was known to all as a commander who demanded much but would go to any length to assure that his men were afforded whatever was needed for their welfare and survival. Larry and I maintained contact as friends after our Vietnam service and after he retired from the Army. Over the years, our friendship grew, and we talked frequently by telephone. In the past few years, we would talk every 1-2 weeks. I was always heartened to pick up the phone and hear a loud, sincere, "Michael, How ya doin'?" He was equally enthusiastic if his call were to be answered by Mary. He knew our children by name, and he inquired about them and our grandchildren with every call. Larry passed away on August 8, 2013. It is a friendship like none other that I've ever had. God bless you, Larry, and thank you.

CONTENTS

ACKNOWLEDGEMENTS

The story of *MISSILE!MISSILE!MISSILE!* would be but a footnote buried in the history of the Vietnam War were it not for the efforts of two wartime comrades and friends, Mike Sloniker and Joe Kline. Mike saw lessons in the story, and while the Army was seeking distance from the memory of Vietnam, Mike doggedly and single-handedly kept the story alive. He is responsible for the transcription of the debrief tape that appears in the appendices of this book. He is also the individual that led the collaboration with Joe in order to see that a visual record of *MISSILE!MISSILE!MISSILE!* would be made to give greater life to the story. Joe, with the assistance of a number of eyewitnesses, through a repetitive trial and error process, achieved a visual depiction of the shoot-down event that captures its terrifying reality with incredible detail. Joe's the ultimate when it comes to Vietnam War aviation art. Without Mike and Joe, this story would likely not have been written. My deepest thanks are extended to both of them.

I am indebted to my comrades in the 229th Combat Aviation Battalion, of the 3rd Brigade (Separate) of the 1st Cavalry Division (later Task Force Garry Owen) for the assistance and encouragement that they have provided me in telling this story. More specifically, my gratitude is unbounded for my friends with whom I served in F Battery, 79th Artillery—the Blue Max. Whatever knowledge and skills that I attained as a pilot could not have happened without their attention and professionalism.

I'm indebted to Bill Wright, the pilot of the rescue Huey and his crew chief, David Vaughn and the rest of their crew for their incredible heroism in pulling Marco and I out of the jungle. Without them, I might not have been here to tell this story.

Most of all, I thank LTC (ret) Larry McKay, to whom this work is dedicated. In addition to his leadership in developing what was recognized as the best Army Aviation unit of its time, he has been my life-long friend. Before his passing in August 2013, he knew of my effort on this story, and he was very supportive and encouraging.

As I've written this story, I've shared it with many of my West Point classmates from the Class of 1966. I'm very grateful for their support and encouragement which has been a primary factor in my continuing this effort to publication.

My daughters, Maureen Peterson and Laura Laumatia were my primary encouragement in continuing to write the story. They were my test audience as I set out to record my thoughts and memories about my experience. Their early interest and enthusiasm prompted me to continue to write and complete the story.

My sisters, Marianne Love and Laurie Tibbs were also among my patient reviewers, and I'm grateful for their encouragement. Brother Jim Tibbs reviewed the story and was moved to provide the illustration in the "On the Ground" chapter of the heroic rescue of Marco Cordon and me. I am extremely grateful to them all.

Finally, it would be normal at this point for me to express my thanks to my wife, Mary. But in this case, my gratitude is more than perfunctory. Mary edits books professionally, and I've prevailed upon her talents in reviewing this work. She did so without charging a fee, and, in the end she pronounced this work readable, coherent, and generally grammatically correct. She also said that she liked it. What more could a guy ask?

INTRODUCTION

A copy of Joe Kline's remarkable painting, which is reproduced on the cover of this book, hangs in the hallway of my home in DuPont, Washington. The painting is the result of a collaboration between Joe and several eyewitnesses to an event that forever changed the lives of me and my copilot and good friend, Marco Cordon.

The life changing event is the shoot-down of the Cobra helicopter gunship which Marco and I were piloting. Joe's painting provides an almost shockingly accurate visual representation of what happened when Marco and I were shot down by a North Vietnamese SA-7 surface-to- air missile near the town of An Loc in South Vietnam on the afternoon of June 21, 1972.

Our survival was improbable and unique. It was improbable because several other Cobras had been similarly engaged by North Vietnamese, and all previous incidents had resulted in the deaths of the crews. It was unique because, to the best of my knowledge, no other helicopter crew has since survived a similar catastrophe.

The location of the painting assures that I see it daily. It is a visual reminder that helps to remind me of the event which occurred more than forty years ago. In truth, I need no reminding. I can say with total certainty that no day has passed since June 21, 1972, in which I have not thought about the event and the people with whom I served. I am eternally thankful to Marco, those who searched for and rescued us, and my comrades in F Battery, 79th Artillery—the Blue Max.

This story recounts how Marco and I survived. But the story doesn't end there. The uniqueness of the story has provided continuing recognition for both of us. That recognition has been uniformly positive, often opening doors that might not have been opened. For me, it has led me to new friends and adventures that I might never have known or experienced.

The experience of the shoot-down has also been an important point of reference in my life's spiritual journey. The meaning of the event has, during the course of my life, has continued to expand in ways that, at the ripe old age of twenty-eight, I couldn't have imagined.

My purpose in this account is to tell that entire story.

I
BLUE MAX

Blue Max, an aerial field artillery unit, was unique. In 1972, it was what was left of a larger unit known as 2nd Battalion, 20th Field Artillery, also an aerial field artillery unit. The larger unit was part of the 1st Cavalry Division (Airmobile). That division, pursuant to the Nixon Administration's Vietnamization strategy, had begun to redeploy from Vietnam during the year prior to my arrival in October 1971. When I arrived, the division's presence had been reduced to a single, separate brigade—3rd Brigade (Separate)--with support units such as 2/20th Field Artillery proportionately reduced in size. F Battery, 79th Artillery was the new designation of what was formerly C Battery, 2nd Battalion, 20th Field Artillery (Aerial Field Artillery).

When I joined Blue Max in mid-October 1971, it had most recently been involved in operations near the Cambodian border northwest of Saigon. The major engagement in those operations was near a firebase called Firebase Pace. After several intense engagements between elements of the 1st Cav and North Vietnamese Army units, the 1st Cav elements were replaced by South Vietnamese Army units (ARVN or Army of Vietnam). Blue Max's continuing involvement in these operations ended as I arrived in country. Indeed, as I was driving to Spokane International Airport to begin my trip to Vietnam, I heard a radio report of a Cobra being shot down northwest of Saigon near the Cambodian border. Soon after my arrival I learned that the Cobra was from Blue Max and that it was piloted by CW2 Ernest Rickenbacker (a cousin of the famed World War I ace, Eddie Rickenbacker) and CPT Jim Maclaughlin.

When I arrived in Vietnam, I did not know that I would be assigned to Blue Max. In fact, I was unaware that such a presumptuously named Vietnam for further assignment. After no more than a day, that situation was resolved. A smiling, wiry, tough looking major with airborne wings, a Combat Infantryman's Badge, Senior Aviator Wings, and a right shoulder Special Forces patch arrived in his jeep at the barracks where I was temporarily billeted and greeted me with, "I'm so pleased to meet you, Super Tiger!" That introduction instantly assured me that I was not heading off to some low intensity, ash and trash outfit.

Like all commanders in Vietnam at the time, Major Larry McKay of Blue Max had an endless task in staffing and developing his unit. One year tours assured a constant, continuing turnover of people, and the then rapid reduction of U.S. Forces in Vietnam complicated the situation even more. Larry was not content to staff with what the system provided him. He had a former classmate friend at Headquarters, USARV (U.S. Army Vietnam) who was in charge of aviation officer assignments. Larry had provided his friend with a profile of the types of officers that he wanted to be assigned to his unit. I was a match for one of the profiles: senior Captain with previous ground combat assignment in Vietnam.

My status as a relatively senior captain would place me in the position of Platoon Commander, 3rd Platoon, F Battery, 79th Artillery (AFA). That position was identified by the radio call-sign, "Blue Max 36." My platoon consisted of four Cobra helicopters and a complementary number of pilots and crew chiefs along with a few other people and equipment assets.

It didn't take me long to learn that I was in a unit that was cloaked with intense pride and obvious and infectious *esprit d'corps*. There was a camaraderie which only comes from mutual respect forged in intense shared experiences. As a new pilot coming into the unit I was immediately impressed, even a bit awed by the high performance standards that were expected of its pilots. These expectations were most commonly articulated by the pilots themselves. Larry McKay was a commander who expected and demanded high professional standards in all aspects of behavior. While fiercely demanding in standards, the unit and its commander were willing to accommodate a learning curve while new pilots trained and gained experience. It wasn't lost on me as I assimilated into Blue Max that this respect and regard extended beyond the unit. "Max" pilots were regarded by those whom they supported with an appreciation that bordered on awe. Such esteem challenged pilots, new and experienced alike, to conduct themselves in ways that truly reflected the unit's high standards and expectations.

2

There is much more that I could say about Blue Max, but it's a subject worthy of its own narrative. Indeed, the unit and its commander, Larry McKay, have been the subject of several television documentaries as well as subjects of frequent mention in a number of written histories, most notably *The Battle of An Loc* by James Willbanks. [1]

---

[1] *The Battle of An Loc*, James Willbanks. Bloomington, Indiana, Indiana University Press: 2005.

II
EARLY TOUR
October 1971-March 1972

BLUE MAX
AREA OF OPERATIONS
1971-1972

Key Locations, Blue Max Area of Operations, 1971-1972

When I arrived for my second Vietnam tour in October 1971, I found a few surprises. I had spent my first tour mostly in the field as an artillery forward observer with an Infantry rifle company in the 1st Infantry Division. That tour was highlighted by the 1968 Tet Offensive and its aftermath. From the moment of my arrival on that tour, the trappings of combat urgency were evident. The bus ride from Bien Hoa Air Base to the 90th Replacement Barracks at Long Binh was undertaken with due regard for the possibility of enroute hostilities, and the physical security was evident. The barracks had the look of being prepared for the eventualities of combat, and the sound of harassment and interdiction (H&I) artillery fire rumbled constantly through the night. My impression upon arriving for my second tour

5

was that everything was much more relaxed. The bus ride was more like riding, say, from Camden to Philadelphia (sometimes a daunting task in its own right). Blast protection around the barracks buildings was in disrepair with the contents of the sandbags spilling from the many holes in the bags. While there was H&I fire during the nights, it sounded much more distant and much less frequent. In retrospect, my observations on arrival probably reflected a much different combat reality than I had experienced during my first tour. As I would learn soon enough, combat activity was much reduced from what I had experienced four years earlier.

A day or two after arriving at the Blue Max base at Bear Cat Base Camp (just east of Bien Hoa on the map), I was given an orientation flight by one of the unit's standardization instructor pilots. I learned that the Area of Operations (AO) for Blue Max included all of what was then referred to as III Corps—an area bounded on the north and west by the Cambodian border, on the east by the Song Be/Dong Ngai Rivers, and on the south by the South China Sea. The area was very familiar to me; I had walked over most of it during my previous tour with the 1st Infantry Division. That experience would serve me well in my new role as a Cobra gunship pilot. Part of the orientation flight was also a check ride which evaluated my flight technique, general flying knowledge, flight safety and emergency procedures, including my proficiency in "touch down" autorotations. I passed.

After initial in-processing, I began to learn more about Blue Max's mission. As an aerial field artillery unit, the unit's mission was principally to provide fire support to infantry units in enemy contact. Aerial field artillery extended the range in which infantry could operate. With conventional "tube" artillery such as 105 mm, 155 mm, and 8-inch howitzer batteries, infantry was constrained to operate within the maximum range of these guns. For example, an infantry unit relying on a 105 mm howitzer battery for its fire support could not operate beyond 11,500 meters—the maximum range of that battery's guns—from the battery's location. Aerial Field Artillery Cobras, providing fire support capability similar to that of a howitzer battery, significantly increased the operating range of the infantry.

Blue Max had several other missions as well. Most common of these were aerial gun escort for troop carrying UH-1H (Huey) troop carrying helicopter formations on combat assaults (we often referred to Hueys as "slicks" as they were armed only with M-60 machine guns at the doors) and escort for medical evacuation Hueys known either as Med-Evacs or Dustoffs. Blue Max maintained a 24/7 "hot section" consisting of two Cobras armed and fueled. The hot section would be the first to deploy in the event of a requirement for fire support for troops in contact or to escort medical evacuation missions. The hot section was required to be airborne within two minutes of notification of such a mission. In the event of the hot section's deployment, a stand-by section would replace the deployed hot section. To my knowledge, there was never an occasion on which the two minute standard was not met.

For several reasons I did not accumulate a vast amount of flying time during the following months. Because of the relatively quiet situation in our area, there simply weren't as many missions to be flown. There were a few missions in which Blue Max was called upon to support troops in contact, but the vast majority of missions were escort missions on which we provided protective cover to flights of UH-1s carrying troops to and from landing zones or pickup zones. Quite a few of our missions were escort missions for Medevacs or Dustoffs. One disturbing aspect of this was that too many such missions were flown in order to remove troops from the field who were experiencing substance abuse issues.

Another reason for my low flight time accumulation was that as a relatively senior captain, I was frequently called upon to perform functions more administrative in nature. Because of the rapid draw-down of U.S. Forces at the time, more bases were either being closed or turned over to the South Vietnamese. This resulted in several relocations of our operations bases. Within two weeks of my arrival in Blue Max, I was given the task of managing the relocation of our unit from Bear Cat Base Camp to a small base called Plantation between Long Binh and Bien Hoa. I would be called upon to perform similar functions on two other occasions during my tour. These were interesting assignments requiring much detailed attention and coordination among a variety of groups.

In late 1971 the comparatively low level of combat involving U.S. forces allowed for a fairly relaxed pace at the various Blue Max base camps. We were able to watch the latest movies from the States almost nightly. Jane Fonda had not yet made her trip to Hanoi, and her movies were still quite popular. There was a basketball court in the area, and I, along with others, spent much time honing my basketball skills. The unit officers' club was well patronized, and it was home to a seemingly endless poker game in which several experienced participants displayed remarkable skill in their methods of instruction to those lesser experienced. As was true in other units, a variety of pets seemed to find a home in our area. Most memorable was a monkey who was creatively named, "Monk." Monk lived near the end of one of the barracks buildings where he was tied. Located near him was an open 55-gallon drum which was used to store water for fire suppression. He seemed well-adapted to his environment as he would chatter loudly and "flip off" passers-by. If that behavior didn't draw the desired attention, he'd throw water or anything else that was handy at his victims before jumping in the barrel and swimming to the bottom to hide.

The comparatively low level of combat that was occurring in our area of operations at the time didn't preclude fairly frequent engagement of our Cobras by enemy gunners. Usually, such encounters involved small-arms fired by the enemy. Most commonly, we were fired upon by AK-47 rifles or light machine guns. On rare occasions, our helicopters would be engaged by enemy 12.7 millimeter[2] heavy machine guns. When that happened, it would involve much conversation with everyone eager to learn the location and circumstances, presumably with the hope of getting in on the action. Overall, though, there was little happening in our area that would suggest the presence of large numbers of enemy forces.

Early in 1972, we began to hear reports that large numbers of North Vietnamese were moving into sanctuary areas just across the Cambodian border from our operations area. Most of these reports

---

[2]Enemy 12.7mm machine guns were often referred to as 51-caliber machine guns. This probably happened because these weapons closely resembled American-made 50-caliber guns. Although technically incorrect, the 51-caliber reference stuck, and the references 12.7mm and 51-caliber were used virtually interchangeably. A battlefield legend had it that the Warsaw Pact purposely settled on the 51-caliber size because it would be capable of firing our ammunition while we couldn't fire theirs. There was a similar situation with 81mm Mortar; the Warsaw Pact version was an 82mm Mortar.

were unattributed; they were often prefaced with something like, Early in 1972, we began to hear reports that large numbers of North Vietnamese were moving into sanctuary areas just across the Cambodian border from our operations area. Most of these reports were unattributed; they were often prefaced with something like, "When I was over at Bien Hoa yesterday, I had lunch with an old friend from flight school. He told me that he'd just heard a report from a Scout Pilot that he'd been flying across the border into Cambodia and that he and those with him could see huge camps of NVA. They were equipped with tanks and trucks and they were in concrete bunkers. There were several sand- bagged anti-aircraft positions with 12.7 mm guns, but they didn't engage us. They know that our rules of engagement prevent us, when we're over Cambodia, from firing on enemy unless we're first fired upon; so, what these guys do is they just stand there looking at us and flipping the bird at us....stupid rules of engagement!" [3]

As January progressed into February and February into March, the frequency of these "rumors" steadily increased. Most of us were aware that there was a massive troop buildup on the Cambodian side of the border. Strangely, we didn't, to the best that I can recall, hear any of this from anyone speaking in an official capacity; rather, it was the stuff of rumors. It may have been rumor, but most of us, especially those with prior experience in the area, assigned them a high degree of credibility.Saturday, April 1, 1972, was the first night of the Easter "truce" for that year. Throughout my first Vietnam tour in 1967-1968, there were a number of similar truces agreed to by the various combatants in the war. All of them were routinely violated by the Viet Cong and the North Vietnamese. Most famous among these violations was the Tet Offensive of 1968. That history is well-known,

_____

[3]In June 2013, a close friend, Dave Ripley, visited me at my home in DuPont, Washington. Dave was a Scout Pilot who flew OH-6A reconnaissance helicopters. He recalled flying numerous missions over the border into Cambodia during this period. He tells of extensive infrastructure development along with the presence of massive numbers of enemy equipment being staged in the sanctuary areas along the border. He also expresses frustration that his reports and the reports of others who were with him seemed to fall on deaf ears—even to the point that he felt that his own credibility was in question.

but my own experience was that, while the scale was usually much smaller than that of Tet '68, military operations by our enemies continued through all such truces. It was not a great surprise, then, when the base siren at Long Thanh North Army Airfield sounded around midnight between April 1 and April 2, signaling a "Red Alert." Other than that tension-building interruption of a relaxing evening, there was no further indication of anything untoward in the vicinity of Long Thanh—no small arms fire, no thump-thump of mortar tubes, no illumination fired by friendlies—just the usual chirping of frogs and the Geckos singing what GI's presumed translated to "FU!"

On the morning of April 2, AFVN (Armed Forces Vietnam) Radio informed us that the North Vietnamese Army (NVA) had crossed the DMZ (demilitarized zone) separating North and South Vietnam. Accounts were variable. There were virtually no U.S. ground troops in the area, so the brunt of the NVA attack was being borne by South Vietnamese Army units. These were reputedly some of the finest units in the South Vietnamese Army (ARVN). Some of the reports, though, were discouraging. There were reports that some ARVN units were fleeing in disarray. Other reports told an opposite story. We also heard of NVA units attacking with large maneuver forces in the open, exposing themselves to easy targeting by U.S. air power. All in all, the reports seemed a pretty mixed bag, and, to us at Long Thanh North, it was a matter of interest, but operations in our area seemed to continue as they had for several months. There was a bit of a feeling that we'd somehow dodged a bullet as the major activity seemed to be in the north, hundreds of miles from our location.

That soon changed.

III
LOC NINH

Loc Ninh during the Vietnam War looked like a town that should have been peaceful. It was small, maybe 10-15 thousand people, mostly Montangards, and it was located along National Highway 13, approximately 10 miles from the Cambodian border. It was surrounded by French-owned rubber plantations, and there was an unmistakable French influence on the appearance of the town—many stucco buildings with red tile roofs. Its elevation was just enough to allow it to be slightly cooler than towns further to the south. Its appearance was pleasant and almost inviting, but it was, in the war's scheme, a victim of its location. Highway 13 crossed the border just north of the town, and it led directly to the sanctuary bases of the North Vietnamese. The location combined with its status as a district capital and home to various South Vietnamese military units made it an inviting and obvious target for various North Vietnamese/Viet Cong military activities.

I first heard of Loc Ninh in 1967, during my first Vietnam tour when I was with the U.S. 1st Infantry Division. The "Big Red One" fought against a combined VC/NVA force at Loc Ninh in October/November 1967, in what history regards as one of the most lop-sided battles of the Vietnam War. Over 1000 VC/NVA were killed in the battle at a cost of four Americans killed. The enemy inexplicably continued "human wave" attacks across an airport runway against a small military compound on the opposite side. During the battle, an American artillery battery from 6th Battalion, 15th Artillery placed 105mm howitzers at one end of the runway and blasted the enemy with direct fire down the runway as the enemy forces crossed it, in human wave attacks.

The artillerymen at the battle employed a type of ammunition called "beehive" rounds in the fight. Beehive was a name for a type of artillery shell that contained thousands of small steel darts that looked like finned nails. It was very effective against personnel in the open, which is exactly what the enemy presented in their attacks.

I was not present at this battle; I heard about it a day or two later.

During my tour, I would spend time in the area around Loc Ninh on infantry patrols, and I found the area to be generally peaceful, quiet, and pleasant.

In April 1972, I would revisit the Loc Ninh area.

By early 1972, the American military presence in Vietnam had been drastically reduced. From a high of 524,500 troops in 1969, the American troop population was reduced to 69,000 by mid-January of 1972. By this time there were virtually no U.S. ground troops remaining in country and all ground operations against the NVA (practically speaking, there were no Viet Cong remaining by this time) were being conducted by the ARVN, the Army of Vietnam. The remaining Americans were largely aviators, advisers, and headquarters and support troops. While aviators were among the last remaining forces, their withdrawal was occurring at an increasingly rapid pace. The practical effect of this is that almost no one in country at the time would be required to serve a complete 12-month tour, the standard tour length in the past. At the unit level, this meant that experienced aviators were being rotated home at a quickening pace.

In Blue Max, as in other Army Aviation units, pilots normally served a lengthy "apprenticeship" period before they were given mission command responsibilities. Nominally, a new pilot with no prior combat aviation experience would serve six months and/or 300 flight hours before he would be considered for aircraft commander. Each Cobra in Blue Max was piloted by an Aircraft Commander and a Co-pilot/Gunner. In more standard parlance, this would be a pilot and a co-pilot. In addition to the esteem that went with being an aircraft commander, there was a more practical aspect. The Cobra was configured with two sets of controls, one in the back seat where the aircraft commander was positioned, the other at the co-pilot/gunner's station in the front seat. The front seat flight controls were extremely difficult to operate; they were designed to allow the co-pilot/gunner to land the aircraft in an emergency or if the aircraft commander were incapacitated, but their difficulty of operation rendered them almost useless for extended periods of flight.

An interesting, perhaps unusual, dynamic of the Aircraft Commander

—Co-pilot/Gunner relationship was occasioned by the fact that Blue Max had several more captains assigned than were standard for the unit. This meant that recently arrived captains would be assigned to fly missions in which they functioned as co-pilot/gunners while the aircraft commander for the mission might be a warrant officer or a lieutenant. Experience and flying skill were given a higher value than rank. Such departures from normal protocols were supported by the commanders of Blue Max, and, to the best of my knowledge, no issues ever resulted from these temporary reversals of the usual roles of rank. In the air, the aircraft commander, regardless of rank, was always king, and everyone accepted that.

As the overall pace of troop withdrawal accelerated in the early months of 1972, pilots who had been functioning as co-pilot/gunners were pushed more rapidly to the role of aircraft commander. In my case, I was designated an aircraft commander after just over four months in country, when I had accumulated 256 flight hours. I flew my first mission as an aircraft commander on March 21, 1972.

On April 5, 1972, I was flying my fifth mission as an aircraft commander. I don't specifically recall the details of that mission, but I do recall that I was flying the second Cobra in a two- ship mission. The lead ship was flown by CW3 Charles Windeler. His co-pilot/gunner was CPT Henry Spengler, a 1968 graduate of West Point. Hank Spengler had only recently been assigned to Blue Max. He, along with several others, had been transferred from the 4th Battalion, 77th Artillery (AFA) of the 101st Airborne Division. The last units of the 101st had been redeployed to the United States, and those pilots who had most recently arrived in country were redeployed within South Vietnam. I believe that Blue Max received all of the pilots that were redeployed from the 4th Bn, 77th AFA. In any case, there were three additional West Point graduates—Dutch Harmeling ('69), Tom Garrett ('69), and Ed Northrup ('68). All of these pilots were Captains.

My best recollection of the mission that I was flying was that we were covering ARVN operations somewhere in the eastern III Corps area— the eastern portion of the Blue Max area of operations.

Early in the afternoon we were notified that we were to suspend our current mission and fly to the vicinity of Loc Ninh. We were given coordinating information such as call signs and frequencies of contacts in the area. We weren't given much specific information as to the nature of our new mission except that we would be supporting troops in contact, and it looked like something significant was developing.

We flew as quickly as possible to Loc Ninh. Because of the distance we may have refueled along the way. If that had been the case, we probably would have refueled at Song Be, about 30 miles east of Loc Ninh. Along the way we began to hear the radio traffic around Loc Ninh. Clearly, a major engagement was taking place. There were several ground contacts with whom we communicated. Most of them had call-signs with variations of "Zippo" in them. We had no way of knowing what their unit structure was, so initially we regarded them all equally. In any case, all of them seemed to have plenty of targets. As we learned more about the ongoing activity, we began to hear of things of which we'd never heard before. Apparently, the NVA were employing tanks and other armored vehicles in the battle along with conventional artillery. We also began hearing of observations of much heavier artillery than was normally found on battlefields in that part of Vietnam. 12.7mm heavy machine guns and 37mm conventional anti-aircraft artillery had been reported. There were even reports of 57mm flak-producing anti-aircraft weapons. Except for the 12.7mm guns, these were weapons with which we had had no experience, and in the case of the 12.7mm, our prior experience had been very slight.

As we reached Loc Ninh, we were joined by another Blue Max flight of two ships. That flight was led by CW3 Barry McIntyre. His wing was

CPT Bill Leach, another like myself who had only recently been designated an aircraft commander. Other than Hank Spengler, I can only recall the name of one other co-pilot/gunner—that would have been WO1 Jim "Jet" Jackson. He may well have been my front seat; 40+ intervening years have fogged that memory.

There is no fog, though, regarding my memory of what happened during that mission. We were given a mission to attack a known anti-aircraft site. It was several kilometers south from the town of Loc Ninh in an indistinguishable area of jungle. All four of our Blue Max birds joined together to form a four-ship, heavy fire team, led by Charlie Windler. I was flying behind Charlie, followed by Barry McIntyre and Bill Leach. Initially, each of us made a rocket run on the assigned target (we could not see the target; we were essentially firing on grid coordinates in otherwise non-descript jungle). All four of us made an initial run, one after another from east to west. On that first run, I could hear automatic weapons fire being fired at my aircraft. From the rate of fire, I believed it to be 12.7mm. I'd been fired upon by such weapons when I was on the ground during my first tour, so I was familiar with their rate of fire. Others in the flight heard the fire also, but we did not see the muzzle flashes at that time. At this point, I can't be certain of what altitude we initiated our attacks, but in previous operations, we'd normally fire our rockets from a fairly shallow dive starting at about 3,000 feet. On that day, after our first pass at the target, we agreed that we would terminate our dives above 3,000 feet out of respect for the heavier weapons which we were encountering.

Charlie Windeler led our second pass as well. I was following him and in my dive when he radioed that we should be alert, that he thought that he and Hank had heard some kind of "clunk" as they were inbound to the target. I responded with a "Roger," and continued my dive. I was probably about to fire when I heard Barry McIntyre in the ship behind me yell into his radio, "Windy! You're on fire! Get it down! Get it down!" I looked up and I could see that the entire exhaust stack on Windy's bird was in flames. There was a clear area slightly to the southwest of our flight path and it appeared that he was attempting to fly to that area. It also appeared that he was flying what would have been a normal, powered approach. I had broken off from my rocket run and was following Windy down, when I heard Barry again, "Windy, Get her down! Get her down!" Windy responded, "I am! I am!" At first the fire appeared to be contained within the exhaust stack, but it soon engulfed the entire rear portion of the helicopter's engine compartment. At this point, it appeared that they began to lose control of the aircraft. They made a fairly slow left turn and came to what appeared to be almost a hover when the fire burned through the tailboom which separated from the aircraft. They then plummeted to the ground and the aircraft exploded. I continued to follow their path. All the while, I was hearing the *thunka-thunka-thunka* of the 12.7mm guns. As I approached 1200 feet, I determined that the anti-aircraft fire was too heavy for me to continue, and I overflew the crash site and began to climb and depart the area. I satisfied myself that there were no survivors. All that remained by this time was a distinct crater surrounded by grey, smoking ash. There was also a vertical, black plume of smoke that extended high into the air.

As I was departing, I saw another Cobra overfly the crash site several hundred feet below me. I remember thinking, "I don't know who that guy is, but he must have balls of iron." Twenty-three years later, while comparing notes and sharing dinner with our wives, I learned the identity of that pilot. He was CPT Ron Timberlake.[4]

The Loc Ninh battle continued for two more days, through the 7th of April when the North Vietnamese succeeded in overrunning all of the ARVN/US compounds and outposts in the town. That it took three days for the NVA to accomplish this can be credited largely to the efforts of one American. This was CPT Mark Smith whom we knew at the time only as "Zippo." Zippo seemed to be everywhere. He was coordinating our helicopter gunships, U.S. Air Force aircraft, directing ground activity and communicating constantly with various command elements flying over his location. In the course of the battle, he was wounded more than forty times. His own account of the battle is a fascinating tale that, if related in a bar room conversation, would stretch credibility to its limits. Having been there through extended portions of the battle, I can vouch for those parts of his account that relate to communications with supporting and aviation elements. It was, and is, my opinion that CPT Smith's performance at Loc Ninh was fully consistent with an award of the Medal of Honor. He did receive a Distinguished Service Cross (2nd highest decoration for gallantry in action). I, along with several others, was a part of a group of Loc Ninh veterans who participated in an unsuccessful effort in the late 1990s to have Smith's DSC upgraded to a Medal of Honor. CPT Smith was able to escape Loc Ninh after it was overrun, but he was captured by the NVA a short time later. His account of the battle and of his captivity can be found on the internet at the following website: <http://www.pownetwork.org/bios/s/s198.htm>.

---

[4]Ron and I would become close friends 23 years later when we found ourselves living near one another in Houston. During that time, Ron wrote a history of Army Aviation involvement in the battles of Loc Ninh and An Loc. His document has served as a well-regarded source document for many subsequent histories of the battles. Ron died in Houston in 1999 as a result of a tragic motorcycle accident.

Loc Ninh was my baptism of fire as a Cobra pilot. After the first day which saw the loss of CW3 Windeler and CPT Spengler, I flew in support of the battle through its conclusion on April 7. On April 7, I established my personal one-day record for flight time at 13.5 hours. During the battle several attempts were planned to rescue the Americans on the ground at Loc Ninh. One of these attempts involved the use of an incapacitating gas called Rum Bay, which was supposed to put everyone on the ground to sleep. Supposedly, the gas would not produce lasting injury to those affected; its only purpose was to incapacitate the enemy long enough that friendly aircraft could land at Loc Ninh and evacuate our Americans (who presumably would also be asleep). Blue Max would provide the gunship support for the helicopters entering the town. In order to do this, we were required to wear our standard issue Army gas masks while flying. In addition to the discomfort of wearing these contraptions while also wearing a flight helmet, normal aircraft communications were severely impaired, as our intercoms and radios relied on microphones mounted on helmet booms that were outside our gas masks. In the end, a single helicopter, an OH-6A, began an approach to the compounds at Loc Ninh only to have its front plexiglass riddled with bullets. So much for incapacitating gas. After this, our rescue effort was terminated, and I don't recall that any others were attempted.

After the Battle of Loc Ninh concluded we were aware that some of the Americans who had been in Loc Ninh might have escaped, and we continued our efforts to locate and rescue them. One of these efforts did result in a successful rescue although the rescued Americans were not from Loc Ninh. Instead they had, under intense and overwhelming enemy pressure, evacuated an ARVN artillery fire support base located south of Loc Ninh in the direction of An Loc. On April 8, CPT Marvin Zumwalt and several others were rescued in one of the most extraordinary combat rescues ever executed by Army Aviation. The pilots were CPT John Whitehead and CPT Dave Ripley. CPT Whitehead passed away recently, and his interment at Arlington is occurring as I write. Dave Ripley has remained a close friend, and he and I correspond frequently, usually to celebrate patriotic holidays and to commemorate our fallen comrades. I will not attempt to provide the details of their valiant rescue; rather, I will refer the reader to Marv Zumwalt's account which can be found on the internet at the following website:

<http://www.229thavbn.com/Rescue-from-Cat-Lo-Bridge.htm>.

Marv's account is well-written and detailed. While recounting what was likely the most terrifying experience of his life, he has managed to incorporate much self-deprecating humor. His story is a great read!

To say that Loc Ninh challenged Blue Max is understatement. Because of the nature of the enemy threat, we had to quickly adapt to new realities, not the least of which was the realization that the enemy was far better equipped to effectively engage our helicopters than he'd ever been in the past. The enemy's heavy anti-aircraft weaponry made flight at any altitude below 5,000 feet risky. We immediately determined that we would "break" from our rocket runs at or above 3,000 feet. This forced us to change our gunnery techniques.

Typically, in the past, we would initiate our rocket runs at about 3,000 feet. We'd then lower the nose of the aircraft about 20 to 30 degrees and align the "pipper"[5] with our target. Rocket motor burnout on our 2.75" Folding Fin Aerial Rockets was about 1,500 meters from launch, leaving the rocket flying a ballistic, unpowered trajectory at greater distances. This allowed an effective horizontal range of about 3,000 meters from a Cobra at 3,000 feet. The effective horizontal range from 4,000 or 5,000 feet is drastically shortened. In order to compensate, it is necessary to fire the rockets from a much steeper angle. We quickly learned to fire our rockets from a dive of about 75 to 80-degrees. This required some new techniques. In engaging a target, we'd fly toward it at about 5,000 feet until it disappeared under the nose of the aircraft. Then we'd slow the speed of the aircraft to about ten knots while maintaining our altitude. When we were at less than ten knots airspeed, we'd steadily push the nose of the aircraft over until reaching about a 75-degree dive. We then had about five

---

[5]The AH-1G had an "infinity reflex sight" at the pilot's station in the back seat. The sight was a transparent plate which was mounted on top of the pilot's instrument panel. When it was armed, a red dot would appear at the center of the plate. This dot would maintain its position regardless of how or where the pilot was sitting. At the point at which, the dot was centered on the target, the rocket pods were also aligned with the target. Pilots referred to the dot as the "pipper." It was quite easy to use, the most essential requisite skill being to point the aircraft at the target....in trim, of course

seconds to line up the pipper on the target and fire our rockets. Longer than five seconds in the dive would risk our exceeding the maximum allowable airspeed (190 knots) for the aircraft. After firing the rockets, we'd then bring the nose of the aircraft back up to horizontal. At this point, we'd feel a "g-load" that was something that most of us had never experienced. (Air Force pilots used to diving jet aircraft will laugh at this!) As the g's increased, the aircraft would begin to shake as it shed its air loading, and we'd sense that we were "mushing" through altitude...that is, the aircraft did not have the power to immediately halt the descent, and it would continue to descend even at near maximum power. After a few seconds, the aircraft would resume its normal flight characteristics, and we'd begin to climb out from our dive to repeat the process again.

All of this was new to us at the time, but it did allow us to fly above the effective fire of the NVA anti-aircraft while maintaining our firing accuracy. One reason that the NVA effectiveness was reduced is that the Cobra is very difficult to see at higher altitudes. The fuselage at its widest point is 36". At 5,000 feet, an optical sight on an anti-aircraft gun is difficult to line up with a target that is only 36" wide.

Loc Ninh was the first of several emotional tests that would confront Blue Max and its pilots. For me, the horror of watching Charlie Windler's and Hank Spengler's crash was something that I would remember forever. They were in full view at my 12 o-clock from the time that they were first on fire until the moment of impact. It was one of those surreal experiences in which one sees what's happening and processes it in a way that hopes for some reason for denial. The reality that there is nothing that one can do except to watch the event to its certain conclusion cloaks one with a sense of utter helplessness. All the while, one asks, "What should I be doing? What can I do?" Afterward, the thought continues: "Did I do everything that I could have done? Did I do enough?" I decided that my best service to the memories of these two fine men was to make sure that the facts surrounding their deaths would not be twisted, changed, or misrepresented.

The essential fact to me was that Windler and Spengler were KIA; they were not MIA. I had watched the crash and its aftermath, and I was satisfied that if there were any possibility of survivors of the crash or people escaping the crash, I would have observed it. Within a couple of weeks, I was interviewed by an investigator, I think from the Department of the Army. I was emphatic with the investigator in expressing my view that classifying these men's status as MIA would be an injustice to them and to their families. My conversation with that investigator was the last official communication that I ever had with respect to Charlie's and Hank's deaths.

For many of us in Blue Max, Loc Ninh represented the first clear-cut, battlefield loss of our experience. In my first tour, in 1967-1968, I was involved in situations in which U.S. Army units lost battles to the NVA/VC; however, in those cases the battlefields were quickly reclaimed or the enemy units were subsequently destroyed. In the case of Loc Ninh, the enemy was able to defeat the defending ARVN forces and their American advisers. There was no reclaiming the location. We vicariously witnessed the transfer of power at Loc Ninh as friendly forces were defeated. We were unable to exert our will to the point that we could rescue our fellow Americans from the battle. Such was an unfamiliar experience to most of us. In the end, the reality was that from April 7, 1972, onward, Loc Ninh was never again occupied by forces friendly to the United States.

For many in Blue Max there was another factor weighing on our emotions. None of us discussed it much, but it was a reality nonetheless. In terms of American involvement in Vietnam, the die had been cast. By 1972, everyone knew that our military involvement was no longer about victory over the enemy. T he real mission was two-fold, one part explicit, the other implied: 1) To provide assistance as necessary to strengthen and develop the Vietnamese military to a point of self-sufficiency, and 2) to provide the security necessary to allow the orderly reduction and redeployment of U.S. military and non-military forces. The stark meaning at the individual level was that dying in service to one's country in such circumstances could not be framed in the same kind of motivation as if one were forfeiting one's life for high national purpose. The intensity that we encountered daily at Loc Ninh, and later at An Loc, served to clarify more personally our relationship to our mission. World War II was the last war in which total destruction of the enemy was the core of the mission. American wars since then have been more restrictive in nature with their purposes more politically defined. Such circumstances inevitably provoke questions and debate about purpose. Soldiers are not immune to such questioning. It is with a great deal of empathy that I consider the circumstances of the soldiers are currently deployed in Afghanistan.

Some one in an earlier war speaking about similar circumstances articulated it well, and I paraphrase: "In the end we were not fighting for our country or other similar noble purpose; in the end we fought for each other." I think that there was much of that kind of thought that bound Blue Max, both internally and with those whom we supported.

IV
AN LOC

With the fall of Loc Ninh, the city of An Loc became the northernmost friendly outpost in the Highway 13 corridor. None of us had any illusions about what the next North Vietnamese initiative would be. By now, we were aware that the size of the force that had been positioned to invade the III Corps area was much larger than was necessary to be singularly occupied with Loc Ninh. The only real question was whether the enemy would direct his main effort against An Loc itself or if he would launch a small diversionary attack against the city, masking a much larger attempt on Saigon itself. An Loc was the only significant "hard point" that would hinder an attack on the Saigon area to the south. Very quickly after Loc Ninh became settled, An Loc began to receive increasing amounts of indirect fire in the form of mortars, rockets, and artillery. The reports of enemy movements in the area around An Loc also increased dramatically. We would not have to wait long in order to learn the enemy's intentions.

The nights of April 11, 12, and 13, were difficult for friendly forces in An Loc. The NVA unleashed barrages of 7,000-10,000 rounds of artillery fire on each night. This was into an area that, in area was approximately 1000 meters by 1500 meters. The city literally became oversaturated with incoming artillery fire. The first major North Vietnamese attack came on April 13. The attack was preceded by a 10,000 round artillery barrage. Early in the morning, I was flying to An Loc leading a section of Blue Max Cobras. When I departed Lai Khe after refueling and rearming, there was no problem locating An Loc. Some 40 miles north of Lai Khe, a thick, black column of black smoke was clearly visible.

Several weeks before this, I awoke late one night from a dream. In the dream, I was flying someplace in Vietnam in a heavy combat engagement. Because of the intensity of the battle, I later surmised that it must have been somewhere in northern South Vietnam— probably in or around the Demilitarized Zone. In the dream there were numerous aircraft involved. It was apparently early in the morning, because the sky was more dark grey than blue. Tracers etched the sky in all directions, and the firing was so heavy that the grey sky took on a pinkish tone. It was surreal....as though it might have been a scene from one of those 1950s action comic books. The visual stuck with me for several days. I assured myself, though, that air combat scenes of that intensity simply didn't happen in South Vietnam.

As I continued flying toward An Loc that morning of April 13, the smoke became thicker and thicker. Somewhere around Chon Thanh, I switched to the radio frequency for the American adviser on the ground. I had no idea who he was. My initial call was answered by someone with one of the slowest southern drawls that I'd ever heard, identifying himself as Tunnel One Zero Alpha. He described his situation to me, and he emphatically told me not to come to An Loc, that the anti-aircraft activity was too heavy for low, slow birds like Cobras and that our ordnance would be too light to handle what he had going on anyway. By this time, I was close enough to An Loc that I could see the Air Force aircraft over the city. Every place that I saw aircraft, I saw anti-aircraft fire. One particular A-37 was flying toward me at about 7,000 feet when I saw a line of green tracers appear to intersect the aircraft at the air intake at its right wing root. Apparently, it was not hit, as it continued to fly. The scene, though, was remarkably similar to the one that I remembered from my dream several weeks earlier....so much for lack of air combat intensity over South Vietnam.

I was not about to argue with Tunnel 10-A, who I later learned was the legendary Colonel Bill Miller. He told me that I needed to get back south and tell the powers-that-be that he needed all the high performance, heavy ordnance bearing aircraft that could be sent and that he needed them soon or, as he put it, "There won't be an An Loc!" I can't remember, but I may well have been the recipient of his famous message, "Send me some Stukas! " [6]

As I reversed course and headed back toward Lai Khe, I wondered whether I had done the right thing. From what I had seen, I certainly had no quarrel with Col. Miller's assessment. Somewhere during the conversations, it became apparent that the NVA had attacked An Loc with a significant number of tanks. By the time that I had returned to

---

[6]Col. Miller and Maj. McKay appeared in a Discovery Channel "Wings" program featuring the Blue Max. In that program, Col. Miller described his telling someone to "Send me some Stukas!" A YouTube video of the program can be seen via a Google video search for "Battle of An Loc."

Lai Khe, High Explosive Anti-Tank (HEAT) rockets had been located for our Cobras. The HEAT rockets were smaller than our standard rockets that carried 17-pound warheads. Their warheads were 10-pounds, a fact that invited questioning about why one would resort to a smaller warhead when attacking tanks. The answer was that HEAT warheads were constructed in such a way that their explosive force was directed and focused in a way that all of the explosive force would be expended in penetrating the armor of the tank. The rounds had a comparatively small bursting radius, but their "shaped" charge was extremely effective against hardened targets or armor. Portable anti-tank weapons such as the World War II era "Bazooka" and the more modern M- 72 LAW (Light Anti-Tank Weapon) employed similar features.

At Lai Khe a section of Blue Max Cobras had been loaded with the HEAT rockets. Piloting one of these birds were CW2 Barry McIntyre and Maj. Larry McKay. Larry was flying as a co- pilot gunner in Barry's front seat. It was one of those situations of which I mentioned earlier where the more senior officer took the more "junior" position in the aircraft. Such was Larry's confidence in his pilots that I can't recall him ever assuming the role of aircraft commander. That expression of confidence, I'm sure, communicated volumes to the pilots in his unit.

CW2 McIntyre and MAJ McKay were soon enroute to An Loc with their section of two Cobras. The second bird was flown by CPT Billy Causey, aircraft commander, and ILT Steve Shields, co-pilot/gunner. When they contacted Tunnel 10-A, Colonel Miller, he tried to wave them off as he had done with me earlier. At this point, NVA tanks had penetrated the An Loc perimeter and were roaming about the streets of the city. One was approaching the command bunker which housed Col. Miller, other American advisers, and the Vietnamese commanders. McKay responded to Col. Miller, that he was armed with HEAT rounds and that he thought that they might be effective in getting the tanks off his back. Because of the risk of friendly casualties, using the heavier ordnance of the Air Force was prohibitive, Col. Miller acceded, and Barry and Larry and their section commenced to attack the tanks. It was a history-making attack marking the first time in the history of warfare that tanks in combat had been destroyed by attack helicopters.

The attack against the tanks amounted to a turkey shoot. The NVA had apparently not trained extensively in combined arms operations, and they allowed their tanks to advance ahead of their infantry. The tank commanders had apparently been told that An Loc had already been won by the NVA, and they rode into town almost as sight-seers with their hatches open and their 12.7mm guns idle as they moved along the streets. At the end of the engagement, the Blue Max Cobras had destroyed 5 NVA tanks.

A few days later, on April 15th, the NVA again attacked the city, again employing tanks. CPT Billy Causey and CW2 Ron Tusi were aircraft commanders in a Blue Max section that destroyed 10 tanks. Ron was described as flying low-level along the streets of An Loc in a hunt for tanks. Apparently, it wasn't a fruitless search. For his actions that day, he was awarded our nation's second highest decoration for valor —the Distinguished Service Cross.

After the attacks of April 13 and 15, the situation at An Loc seemed to stabilize with the enemy holding much of the north half of the city. The city remained surrounded and under siege throughout the remainder of the month and beyond—into June. Resupply could only be conducted by air. The considerable anti-aircraft arrayed around the city—9 battalions worth— made helicopter flights in and out extremely risky. In addition to the anti-aircraft fire, the enemy seemed to have zeroed in his mortars on all possible landing sites. With much technical effort and trial and error, the Air Force was able to devise methods of providing resupply via accurate parachute drops.

For Blue Max, An Loc was a daily affair. Every day for the remainder of April and into the first days in May, Blue Max Cobras would be flying some type of support for An Loc. After April 15, there were no major attacks on the city; however, there was a more or less constant level of incoming artillery. The ARVNs, with a few exceptions, were in a virtual standoff with NVA who maintained hostile pressure against the shrunken An Loc perimeter. To the south of An Loc, the ARVN 21st Division had been redeployed from the Mekong Delta, a relatively quiet area of the country during the Spring Offensive, to advance along National Highway 13 to engage dug-in NVA forces blocking ground access to An Loc from the south. The 21st Division troops advanced as far as Chon Thanh before stalling and becoming engaged in their own standoff with the NVA.

During this time Blue Max missions were usually to provide fire support for troops in contact for the 21st ARVN, to escort U.S. and/or VNAF (Vietnam Air Force)[7] troop lifts in combat assaults, to provide attack support on point targets such as anti-aircraft sites, fortifications, and vehicles, and to escort supply and medical evacuation missions. Probably the most difficult of the missions were the combat assault escort missions. These would typically assign a heavy section (3 Cobras) to escort a flight of five UH-1H troop carrying helicopters— which were referred to as "slicks"—as they would carry troops to assault a landing zone. During the An Loc battle, most of these combat assaults were carried out under fire. Usually , the slicks would be fired upon as they approached or departed from a landing zone (LZ). Often the NVA would be firing mortars into the LZ as the slicks were dropping off their troops. As a Cobra pilot, I marveled at the kind of courage that it required for the slick pilots to maintain their positions in flight and to hold their positions on the ground in order for all troops to be discharged while under such fire. The slick pilots who flew such missions have always had my total respect and admiration.

That being said, I have to admit that I have been surprised and gratified to hear in later years from slick pilots who would express with obvious conviction, "I'm alive today because of Blue Max."

Combat assaults required a great deal of coordination and planning. Before an assault on an LZ, there was often a heavy Air Force and artillery preparation of the LZ and its surroundings. This usually consisted of bombs, including cluster bomb units, dropped by either U.S. Air Force or VNAF aircraft. This would be followed immediately by as many as several hundred ounds of 105mm and /or 155mm howitzer rounds fired into the LZ. The idea was to have the slicks on approach to the LZ precisely at the moment that the artillery

---

[7]Unlike the U.S., the South Vietnamese military assigned all aircraft, be they fixed or rotary wing, to the Vietnamese Air Force (VNAF). The U.S. assigned the bulk of its helicopters to the U.S. Army. This provided the U.S. Army with its own aviation assets to support a variety of helicopter missions, including troop lift, resupply, attack helicopter fire support, and heavy lift for equipment and material relocation. In the South Vietnamese military, all such missions were handled by the VNAF.

preparation fires were lifted. Occasionally, the escorting Blue Max helicopters would fire rockets into the LZ as they flew alongside the approaching troop-carrying slicks. By this time, there was no pretense of suprise; if there were enemy in the area, they were fully aware of what was going on. Such was often the case during the An Loc campaign.

There were many factors that could, at the last minute, affect such operations. The most usual was weather. April was a transitional period in the annual weather pattern in South Vietnam. It was between the extremely dry periods of January and February and the extremely wet periods of July and August. Often, when an early morning combat assault was scheduled, we'd find that the LZ would be obscured by a thick blanket of fog. That would inevitably result in the entire operation being postponed in successive one-hour increments. Blue Max pilots along with the escorted slick pilots would thus be required to remain in our forward staging area, which was usually at the Lai Khe base camp. These idle waiting periods gave us ample time to consider what we were doing and the risks that our missions posed. The reality of the risks of such missions wasn't lost on us, and the waiting, sometimes for 2-3 hours, to kick off a mission could be tortuous. Occasionally during these interminable waits, I'd develop a nausea that I'd quietly keep to myself. Discussing this years later with some of my former comrades, I found, with some relief to my pride, that others suffered the same malady—even to the point of vomiting back in the bushes and out of sight. There was a very real appreciation of the possibility that all among us might not be returning from these missions.

As the weather could be a hindrance to our operations, it also provided us with some benefit. Our respect for the newly acquired anti-aircraft capabilities of NVA forces resulted in our conducting our gunship attacks from higher altitudes than we had before the NVA offensive. Above 3,000 feet, we were still well within the the effective range of most NVA anti-aircraft artillery, but we did provide smaller silhouettes before the NVA gunners. Given the numbers of NVA soldiers on the ground carrying small arms, we calculated that our odds were better at altitude. Coupled with this was the fact that, usually by mid-morning, the fog that blanketed the ground had risen to become a stratum of small, puffy clouds at about 3000 feet. These clouds were large enough to provide some cover as we flew in airspace above anti-aircraft concentrations.

There were some occasional difficulties with this tactic. Activities at An Loc attracted a lot of aircraft. I don't know if anyone ever attempted a tally on the number of aircraft that were in the air around the city at any one moment, but it sometimes became apparent that there were more aircraft than clouds available in which to hide. The air support included aircraft from all services plus the VNAF. Complicating the issue even more was the multiplicity of types of aircraft, ranging from helicopters to jet fighters to the U.S. Air Force's Spectre (AC-130) gunships. On one occasion, I can recall inadvertently exiting the protective cover of a cloud to see a Navy jet streaking in a dive at my 12 o'clock. It was close enough that I could clearly see the pilot's white helmet, though I couldn't quite make out his name stenciled above the face shield. I think it said he was a Lieutenant.

Another vivid cloud-hopping recollection involves an AC-130 "Spectre" gunship. The AC-130 was a C-130 cargo aircraft modified to the point that it was like an airborne armory. It was equipped with a variety of high rate of fire weapons including 7.62 mini-guns and 20mm cannons. The *pièce de résistance* of its armament, however, was the modified 105mm howitzer that it carried. Classmate Mike Wynne, at the time, a young Air Force officer was apparently instrumental in this remarkable adaptation of this Army weapon to an Air Force platform.

An ARVN Airborne Brigade had been inserted onto a terrain feature called Windy Hill. Windy Hill was located about 4 kilometers southeast of An Loc, and the Airborne Brigade's mission was to advance to the south side of An Loc in order to engage the NVA blocking access to the city from the south. Unfortunately, the Airborne Brigade didn't have to move the 4 kilometers in order to engage the enemy; they were engaged by the NVA immediately on their arrival on Windy Hill. They were a tough bunch, though, and they pushed the NVA back for several days before linking up with the ARVN in An Loc. I flew missions in support of their fight for several days. Their American adviser's call sign was Tiger 36. Only recently, I earned that Tiger 36 was a West Point Class of 1970 Lieutenant by the name of Ross Kelly. I learned of his identity through his recent obituary.

While flying in support of Tiger 36, I couldn't help admiring his tenacity and his coolness under what I knew had to be the most difficult of combat conditions. I have no doubt that this young man's courage under fire had much to do with the success of the Vietnamese Airborne in their breakout from Windy Hill. Others seemed to share my opinion as he was subsequently awarded the Distinguished Service Cross.

One morning, while supporting Tiger 36, I'd been temporarily put on hold. As usual, under such circumstances, I preferred to await my call enshrouded by the protective cover of a convenient and nearby cloud. At one point, I found myself inadvertently exiting the cloud and into likely visual contact with North Vietnamese gunners on the ground. Luckily, there was, at my 12 o'clock, another cloud to which I made a bee-line.

Immediately after I entered the second cloud, I received a radio call from Specter, the AC-130 gunship that I knew to be orbiting at 10,000 feet. The voice on the radio resounded with all the authority that a guy flying around with a 105mm howitzer in back might be expected to project: "Blue Max 36, this is Specter." I responded, "This is Blue Max 36." "36, this is Specter; be advised that you just flew through my gun-target line." What does one say in response to a message like that? I think I just said, "Roger!"

Once in a while in combat, one has a chance to project oneself into the mind of an individual enemy soldier. Such an encounter was presented to me one morning while I was escorting a flight of American slicks preparing to insert ARVN reinforcements into An Loc. This would have been shortly after the NVA had encircled and penetrated An Loc during the attacks of April 11 and April 15.

It was one of those missions that was scheduled to to kick off at something like 8:00 a.m., but it was delayed. We were to escort slicks from the 229th Assault Helicopter Battalion as they carried ARVN troops from Lai Khe to An Loc. We'd fly at something like 5,000 feet to an area just south of An Loc where the slicks would descend rapidly in a spiraling corkscrew descent until they were at tree top level over a massive rubber plantation that bordered An Loc to the south. After that, we'd fly to a soccer field in the city where the ARVNs would be discharged from the slicks, and the slicks would exit the city, flying low level over the rubber trees before climbing back up to 5,000 feet for the return to Lai Khe, where they'd pick up another group of ARVNs.

For some reason, probably weather, the operation was delayed for an hour or so. This meant that we were in the classic "hurry up and wait" mode on the Lai Khe air strip. Such delays were the stuff that provided the idleness that tempted all the "what-ifs" that inevitably circulated through the minds of so many of us as we awaited the order to finally crank up and go. Lots of cigarettes were smoked and lots of butterflies wrenched in the abdominal regions. In retrospect, I think that more than a few of us developed an understanding of what many of our fathers experienced as they sat in their LSTs approaching Normandy on D-Day.

After an hour or so, we were given the go-ahead, and the slicks with our Cobras escorting them took off and climbed to altitude for the trip to An Loc. As we approached the city, we learned that the soccer field was receiving incoming mortar fire. The slicks would not be able to land. With the hope that the enemy mortar attack on the soccer field might end soon, we continued our flight to the point that we were flying at tree top level over the rubber south of An Loc. The slicks were told to fly a holding pattern over the rubber while the situation was evaluated.

Rubber trees in the French plantations in Vietnam are planted in a pattern that is similar to the pattern employed in placing grave markers in military cemeteries. The trees are evenly spaced on a grid in such a manner that they form rows and columns at right angles and also at 45-degree angles. The separation between the trees is such that it allows the development of a very consistent, uniform canopy. There is nothing distinctive to the eye in this canopy; there are no landmarks, and flying over it is very much like flying low level over a flat expanse of water. The lack of visual reference makes it very difficult to locate one's position. It wasn't very long before I was aware that I had no idea exactly where I was except that I was over a rubber plantation—probably a rubber plantation that was full of NVA soldiers. Bordering the rubber plantation to the south and west was a large area that had been defoliated and Rome plowed. [8]

It soon became apparent to me that the leader of the flight of slicks didn't have any better idea of his location than I did. The entire formation was simply flying west over the rubber. Eventually, we reached the edge of the rubber, and the slicks were immediately over an open, Rome-plowed area. The lead made a quick turn to the right in order to return to the relative safety of being over the rubber where it would be more difficult for enemy gunners to spot his flight. Almost as he began his turn, I saw tracers coming from a spot in the Rome-plowed area aimed at the #4 bird in the slick formation. Immediately, I heard, "#4 taking fire! #4 taking fire!" The tracers were coming from a machine gun position which was fortuitously exactly at my 12 o'clock. I gently lowered the nose of my Cobra in order to engage the position with rockets. I was no more than 200-300 meters from the position, and I would have to break from my rocket run very close to the enemy gunner's position. As I aligned my sight with the target, I gently squeezed the trigger button on my cyclic, and NOTHING HAPPENED! There had been an electrical failure in the firing system for my rockets. I told my copilot/gunner to fire his turret mounted 40mm grenade launcher, and the result was the same: NOTHING HAPPENED! Now we were a totally unarmed helicopter about to overfly a bad guy with a machine gun! t would be like shooting fish in a barrel! I'm not sure whether we actually overflew the position; we broke hard to the left, and skedaddled as fast as we could.

Remarkably, the bad guy never fired at us. I was somewhat at a loss

[8]Throughout most of the U.S. involvement in the Vietnam War there was an ongoing defoliation activity called Operation Ranch Hand. The idea was to chemically defoliate large areas of jungle in order to eliminate cover that could be exploited by the enemy for concealment. The chemical used was locally referredto as Agent Orange, presumably because of the orange bands that were painted around the drums that were used for shipment and storage of the material. After an area was defoliated, it would sometimes be Rome plowed. This refers to bulldozer mounted plows that would be employed to knock over the trees in a specified area. The plows were so named because they were manufactured in Rome, Georgia. During my first tour in Vietnam which I spent with the Infantry, I had spent time in defoliated/Rome plowed areas. They were quite open; however the tangle of tree trunks, branches, and underbrush made foot travel through these areas very difficult. The jungle and tropical forests along National Highway 13 which traversed the 60 miles between An Loc and Saigon had been defoliated and Rome plowed to 1,000 meters on either side of the highway.

to understand this, but I later reasoned that this particular gunner, after seeing a Cobra bearing down on him and not firing, must have figured that it was his lucky day, that he'd encountered an unusually charitable Cobra pilot. He simply returned the favor.

Apparently, this is not a unique occurrence in combat. I recently shared this story with a retired Marine Corps Sergeant Major neighbor. He told me of an occasion in the Korean War in which he was in a heavy engagement against attacking Chinese at the "Frozen Chosin." During the engagement, a Chinese soldier was charging his position, and my friend had a perfectly aimed shot at the attacking soldier when his rifle jammed. My friend knew that his war would soon be over, but the enemy soldier, rather than shooting him, simply ran by his position. My Marine friend said he simply sat down and cried.

I suppose that it's, at once, a travesty and a blessing that, in the end, wars actually turn out to be fought by human beings.

After the April 15 NVA attack at An Loc, the situation settled, more or less, into a kind of routine. The NVA had been badly mauled, mostly by U.S. Air, including several massive B-52 strikes. They had been frustrated also by the unexpected tenacity of the ARVN defenders in An Loc. T he remainder of April and early May were characterized by ongoing siege activities in which the NVA continued a steady artillery bombardment of the city, inflicting continuing destruction (by this time, there were few buildings left standing) and a mounting number of ARVN and civilian casualties.

An Loc remained cut off from any kind of over land support. Troop replacement, medevac, and logistical support could only be provided by air. The daily routine for Blue Max included escorting American and VNAF helicopters supporting this effort. Virtually 100% of these efforts were engaged by NVA anti-aircraft fire. Life on the ground in An Loc grew increasingly difficult. In his book, The Battle of An Loc, James Willbanks writes that "one adviser put the odds for surviving outside in the open at 'only 50-50.'" [9] Other accounts tell of shortages of medical supplies that were so acute that Vietnamese civilians occupied themselves by removing the threads from sandbags for use as surgical thread.

---

[9]The Battle of An Loc, James H. Willbanks, p. 98. Indiana University Press, 2005

An Loc after repeated North Vietnamese shelling. Virtually every building in the city was destroyed by the nightly shelling which featured artillery barrages of up to 10,000 rounds.

I don't think that anyone had previously considered the nature of the tasks required of Blue Max during the An Loc battle. Whenever the enemy threw something new at us, we were able to adapt. New and different anti-aircraft weaponry from the enemy drove us to devise and implement different tactics. No one was ever taught in Cobra school to fire rockets from 80-degree dives. "High overhead" approaches were not something that we had practiced at staging fields in the States. The unit had an tremendous capacity for creative adaptation to new and changing realities on the battlefield. Much of that occurred because of the superior leadership with which Blue Max was richly blessed.

Larry McKay, Blue Max 6, had done well in taking an assertive role in staffing his unit. It didn't stop there. He set very high standards for the commissioned officers and warrant officers in the unit. The relaxed standards of behavior that were allowed in some units weren't tolerated in Blue Max. At the same time, we who served under Larry quickly became weren't aware that he would "go to the mountain" on our behalf. One incident that I've never confirmed but I believe to be true involved a situation where one of our crews was returning from An Loc with a badly shot-up bird. It was on final approach to Lai Khe when the engine failed. The pilot auto-rotated to what would have been a safe landing but for an inopportunely placed fence which caught the skids of the Cobra as it was about to touch down. Also, the ground was not level, and the bird tipped onto one side causing further damage. The damaged Cobra would have to be shipped to a rear area maintenance depot for repairs. Somewhere in the surrounding discussion the possibility of fuel starvation came up. For those not familiar with aircraft accident investigations, they can sometimes seem like the conclusion is "pilot error" unless unequivocally proven otherwise— innocent until proven guilty just doesn't apply here. In any case, the Cobra was sling-loaded beneath a CH-47 Chinook helicopter for transport back to the rear area at Bien Hoa Air Base. Apparently, Larry had had some conversation with the CH-47 crew while they were rigging the Cobra for transport. Serendipitously, the rigging securing the Cobra beneath the transporting CH-47 failed just as they crossed the center of the Dong Ngai River a few kilometers from Bien Hoa. A good guess would hold that the Cobra is still in its watery grave today.

Leadership was a quality not limited to the commissioned officers in the unit. Indeed, one of the best combat leaders that I ever encountered was one of our warrant officers, Ron Tusi. Ron was on his fifth Vietnam tour. He began his military career as a Navy corpsman. He subsequently became a Navy Underwater Demolitions Technician (UDT was the precursor to today's SEALs), and later transferred to the Army in order to fly helicopters. He had had at least one previous tour as a Cobra pilot, and he had served as a Cobra instructor pilot in the States. In short, he was a very experienced, well-qualified Cobra pilot. Ron's clear mastery of the Cobra helicopter, along with his leadership ability and combat performance led to his induction to the U.S. Army Aviation Hall of Fame in 1983.

In my two tours in Vietnam War, I don't think that I ever encountered an individual with the coolness under fire that characterized Ron Tusi. His confident, calm professionalism on the radio as he repeatedly led flights of troop-carrying Hueys with Cobra escorts into the An Loc cauldron was a settling influence for many a nervous young pilot.

Another "go-to" warrant officer that stepped up for leadership of these difficult missions was CW2 John (Tony) White. Tony was another Blue Max legend. His route to Blue Max was through Army Special Forces. Early in his career, he had been a pilot for Air America, flying C-47s in Laos early as 1962. Like Ron, Tony was motivated to enroll in the Army flight program by a desire to fly helicopter gunships in combat.

V
SURFACE-TO-AIR MISSILES

Rodney (Rod) Strobridge was a fellow that I wanted to know better. He came to Blue Max, I think, in late March or some time in April of 1972. He was a fairly senior captain, and he'd had a prior Vietnam tour in which he flew fixed wing reconnaissance aircraft. The thing that impressed me about Rod was that he always seemed so relaxed and cheerful. To this day I carry a mental image of him. He was inclined toward chubby, but not excessively so, and he always had a smile....always. It wasn't a forced smile; it was the smile of someone who was comfortable in his own skin, and he wanted others to feel the same. His cheerfulness was a counterpoint to the tension that was continuing to build in Blue Max as the An Loc battle continued with no real end in sight. He was a fellow whose companionship I sought whenever we were in our base camp environment. I honestly don't remember whether we ever flew together; I don't believe that we did.

Robert J. (Bob) Williams had also served previously in Vietnam. He was a very experienced Cobra pilot, and he was slated to become Blue Max's Standardization Instructor Pilot (SIP). In a prior Vietnam tour, he'd been an instructor pilot at the Cobra transition course in which previously qualified helicopter pilots would train for re-qualification as Cobra pilots. He'd had both combat and instructor experience, and he was highly regarded as an uncommonly skilled and experienced Cobra pilot. With my total hours approaching something like 300 as opposed to his more than 2000, I have to say that the prospect of flying with him was mildly intimidating. Whether he felt so or not, to me, that prospect assumed the aura of a "check ride." At this point, I don't recall whether we ever flew together—we probably did—but if we did, I can't recall that the experience was anything like what I feared. A part of Bob's aura was that he was very quiet. He was not given to the games of oneupmanship that would occasionally surface among a group of young stud pilots. He seemed to be content to let his flying do his talking for him. In any case, Bob's obvious competence and experience helped him to "fast track" to aircraft commander at a time when such talents were desperately needed.

On May 11, the North Vietnamese launched their third division-sized assault on An Loc. This assault, like those that preceded it, featured an intense preparatory artillery barrage during the previous night, and the attack was, once again, spearheaded by tanks. By this time, the ARVN had become quite proficient in their use of the American-supplied M72 LAW (Light Anti-tank Weapon), and they were able to blunt the effectiveness of the tanks. It helped that, once again, the North Vietnamese displayed a fatal lack of understanding of how to integrate armor and infantry operations. The tanks, as in their previous attacks, quickly left their infantry support behind.

May 11 was one of those transitional days between the dry season and the rainy season on which the balance favored the rain. The weather around An Loc on that day was cloudy with fairly low overcast, and that affected aviation operations. In order to maintain visibility requirements, aircraft were forced to fly under cloud ceilings in the 3,000 to 4,000 foot range.

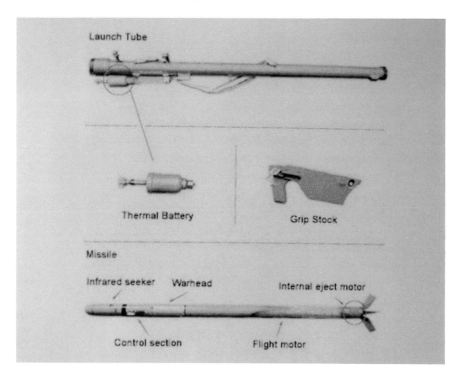

SA-7 Surface-to-Air, Shoulder Launched Missile with Launch Tube, Battery, and Hand Grip

This situation provided significant advantages to North Vietnamese anti-aircraft gunners. Another advantage to the NVA was that, for the first time, they would employ SA-7 "Strella" or "Grail" surface-to-air missiles.

Until this time, there had never been any serious discussion among Blue Max pilots about the possibility of encountering SAMs in our operations. We certainly did discuss much about other, more conventional types of anti-aircraft fire—we were seeing it on a daily basis. However, the subject of missiles was overlooked, either consciously or unconsciously. We had had no training for flying in environments where missile attacks were a threat, and we had little, if any, technical information about North Vietnamese missile capabilities.

Bob Williams and Rod Strobridge were aircraft commander and copilot/gunner, respectively, in a Cobra that was part of a heavy fire team (3 Cobras) supporting the defense of An Loc on the 11th of May. Accounts of what happened are unclear, but what we do know is that they were the first known aircraft and crew to be downed by an SA-7 at An Loc. I have read one account by a Dustoff (call sign of a medical evacuation helicopter unit) pilot who states that his Huey was being escorted by Bob and Rod when suddenly there was an explosion near his aircraft, and Bob and Rod's bird had literally disappeared. Other accounts reported seeing a missile which left a white, corkscrew smoke signature as it struck their aircraft near the engine exhaust pipe and severed the tail-boom. Some of these accounts tell that after the tail-boom was severed, their aircraft went into a descending flat spin. What happened at the end of the descent is unclear, and most reports state that the impact of the helicopter was not observed by any friendly forces. There are a few reports that the aircraft exploded upon impact.

What is clear is that all of this occurred at a time of extremely complex and intense activity, all complicated to some extent by less than ideal weather conditions.

I was not in the area at the time of the Williams/Strobridge shoot-down. I don't recall specifically where I was that day, but I do recall meeting and de-briefing other pilots returning from An Loc that evening. The information coming back was very confusing. Actual eyewitnesses to the shoot-down were hard to come by. There seemed to be much agreement that the shoot-down was the result of a missile strike. Though there was general agreement about a severed tail-boom, finding someone who had actually seen this was difficult. Those who had observed the flat spin descent of the aircraft spoke as if they'd only had fleeting glimpses of the descent. In the discussions, there was one crew that even stated that apart from this incident, they'd seen an SA-2 fired at another aircraft. It was a very confused situation .[10]

Sorting out the confusion did not become any easier when discussing the situation with higher level intelligence people. It seemed that there was a sort of vested interest on the part of higher headquarters in proving that no missiles were present in the An Loc area. Written intelligence summaries avoided mention of missiles in the shoot-down, even to the extent that they speculated that the Williams/Strowbridge Cobra might have been brought down by a B-40 Rocket. [11] The idea that a rocket with a maximum effective range of about 150 meters had been used to shoot down an aircraft in flight at an altitude of 3000 feet was, of course, preposterous, but it does illustrate a curious level of skepticism on the part of our intelligence folks. Such speculation did little to enhance the credibility of our intelligence resources with aviators flying at An Loc.

Soon after the Williams/Strobridge shoot-down, the apparent higher headquarters skepticism toward the idea of surface-to-air missiles seemed to soften. The narrative changed to allow the possibility that there were some SA-7 missiles in South Vietnam. As a precaution against something that continued to be regarded as improbable, we aviators were provided with some basic information about the SA-7.

[10]The SA-2 was a much larger anti-aircraft missile in the North Vietnamese arsenal. It was well known to Air Force and Navy pilots who flew missions in North Vietnam. Because of its size and shape, pilots had dubbed it "the flying telephone pole." It was vehicular mounted or fired from prepared sites. There was never, to my knowledge, any independent confirmation of SA-2s being present in the An Loc area.

[11]The B-40 Rocket was the rocket component of an anti-tank system called the RPG-2. It was man portable and shoulder launched. It had a maximum effective range of approximately 150 meters. It was often used by North Vietnamese troops when attacking troops in bunkers or against vehicles.

aviators were provided with some basic information about the SA-7. We learned that it was man-portable and shoulder- fired. We learned that it could be effective to altitudes as high as 10,000 feet, and we learned that its speed was somewhere around Mach 1 or greater. The missile was guided by an on- board infrared homing device (heat-seeking). Overall, the information that we had indicated a missile roughly comparable to the U.S. made Redeye Missile.

The introduction of missiles to the An Loc battlefield was a particular challenge to helicopter pilots in general, and Blue Max in particular. The missile did not present as difficult a problem for Air Force and Navy jets. Because of the missile's short range (about 3.5 kilometers), jet aircraft—even those traveling at slower speeds than the missile—can be in and out of the missile's effective range when the missile's rocket motor fuel is exhausted. Helicopters have no such advantage. Blue Max Cobras routinely flew at speeds between 120 and 140 knots (140 mph to 160 mph). UH-1H Hueys or slicks flew at a maximum speed of 120 knots. Helicopter pilots had no hope of outrunning a missile that was traveling nearly 800 mph.

What the introduction of the SA-7 missile did for the North Vietnamese was that it gave them the capability of neutralizing helicopter threats at all altitudes. Previously, NVA anti-aircraft was able to threaten helicopters operating at nap-of-the-earth or treetop level with small arms, including individual AK-47 assault rifles and a variety of light machine guns. Above treetop levels, the North Vietnamese could engage with heavier machine guns such as the 12.7 mm discussed earlier. Additionally, the NVA possessed a number of types of anti-aircraft cannons that were supplied by various Warsaw Pact countries. Among these were the 23mm cannon, the 37mm cannon, the ZSU 57 (57mm) vehicular mounted cannon.

Some of these weapons were radar controlled. The accuracy of these weapons against Blue Max Cobras deteriorated noticeably above 3000 feet in altitude. The addition of the SA-7 to the NVA arsenal effectively threatened helicopter flight from the treetops to 10,000 feet.

Under normal circumstances, Cobras could not be flown at altitudes above 10,000 feet, and the effectiveness of the optical sights for the Cobra weapons systems limited our maximum practical maximum altitude to about 6,000 feet. Practically speaking, there was no altitude available to Blue Max pilots at which it was possible to escape the threat of North Vietnamese anti-aircraft fire.

In terms of evasive actions available to helicopter pilots, there were no viable options. There were "suggestions" about what one might do, but such suggestions were communicated as possibilities to be attempted as opposed to known remedies. One of the most common was to, upon learning that a missile had been fired, immediately fly to the treetops in order to attempt to break the infrared "lock" on the horizon. Given the speed differential between the Cobra and the missile, that suggestion was never regarded as practical.

In a business in which we as U.S. Army Aviators were accustomed to the idea that we had been trained to respond to any possible flight emergency, the realization grew that we were now in an environment characterized by the very real threat of emergency situations with no known countermeasures or emergency procedures. The effect on unit morale was like the elephant in the room that everyone knows is there but no one dares to mention. There were, however, some individual behaviors that reflected the tenor of the emotional response.

One evening after supper in our unit base at Long Thanh North, I recall walking outside and observing one of our pilots standing over a small fire that he had built in a shallow pit outside his hooch. In his hand, he held a stack of papers that looked like hand-written letters. I can't remember if we exchanged any words, but he did look up at me and there was, I think, a silent communication between us. He was burning his letters from his wife.

VI
ALONG HIGHWAY 13

A 229ᵗʰ Aviation Battalion Huey inserts South Vietnamese troops along Highway 13 south of An Loc. An abandoned, disabled North Vietnamese tank is in the background.
(Photo by Chad Richmond, used with permission)

After the failed massive NVA attack on An Loc during the period May 11-15, there were no additional division-sized attacks. Once again, the siege settled into a fairly static situation with the ARVN slowly expanding their perimeter and the NVA continuing to apply sufficient pressure to prevent any significant breakout of the ARVN from its besieged positions.

During the same period, a relief effort had been mounted along Highway 13 to the south of An Loc. The ARVN 21st Division from the Mekong Delta was attempting to advance from the town of Chon Thanh along the highway toward An Loc. The ARVN was blocked by well dug- in troops of the 7th NVA Division. The ARVN progress was painfully slow and what progress there was was measured in feet and yards rather than miles. The developing battle of attrition also produced horrendous casualties on both sides.
Blue Max operations had largely shifted from supporting An Loc to supporting the relief effort along Highway 13. These operations were intensely tedious. The NVA 7th Division was well supported by anti-aircraft batteries. The center of mass of their command and

43

control seemed to be around the hamlet of Tan Khai which was located along the highway about six miles south of An Loc. On one occasion, I was given a mission to engage an anti-aircraft battery in the village. It had been firing on our helicopters and other aircraft.

I did engage the anti-aircraft site. It was located, as closely as I could determine, in the center of Tan Khai. My engagement of this anti-aircraft site did not come without considerable emotional investment.

In late 1967 and early 1968, I was an artillery forward observer with an infantry company in the First Infantry Division. The infantry company was C Company, 1st Battalion, 26th Infantry. At the time, the company was operating from a patrol base called Thunder IX along Highway 13. Thunder IX was about a mile south of Tan Khai; we were close enough that we could occasionally hear the activities of village life at night. On a couple of occasions, our company performed what were called "Med-Cap" operations in Tan Khai. Such operations were, in my opinion, one of the most successful outreaches that we had with the Vietnamese people at the time. Our company would patrol before dawn to the village and surround it, "sealing" it in order to prevent anyone from entering or leaving the village. We did this in what I considered a very respectful manner, taking care to avoid property damage and doing our best not to unnecessarily display disrespect toward the villagers. The idea was that any Viet Cong who might have entered the village during the night would have been trapped. As Viet Cong who might have entered the village during the night would have been trapped. As daylight came to the village, we would bring in military doctors and dentists....and intelligence specialists. The doctors and dentists would set up a temporary field clinic and invite any of the villagers in need of medical/dental treatment to avail themselves of the services. Such activities appeared to be quite popular among the villagers, and their expressions and body language clearly communicated that these outreach efforts were very much appreciated. While all this was going on we troops who were not directly involved in manning the perimeter kids. We always carried an ample supply of whatever candy bars we could get, and I think we were pretty effective at winning a lot of hearts and minds. Tan Khai had definitely left its emotional imprint upon me.

Med-Cap" in Tan Khai in late 1967. Gathering of adults in the background is observing a U.S. Army Dentist treating a villager. I was assigned as an artillery forward observer with C Company, 1st Battalion , 26th Infantry, First Infantry Division at this time. This was a "chocolate bar moment."

There was little choice in engaging the anti-aircraft site that I described. I had a profound sense of injustice concerning the actions of the North Vietnamese as they placed their weapons in a location to which I felt such familiarity and attachment. Tan Khai had been occupied for several weeks by the North Vietnamese, and I prayed and hoped that the civilians who had been so friendly to me and my comrades a few years before had by now found some degree of safety from the evil that was being visited upon them. I fired my rockets into the village at the point where the anti-aircraft guns were located. I have no way of knowing whether my rockets were effective in destroying the target or whether any "collateral" damage was done. There were no friendly forces at the location who could report.

The above-described engagement at Tan Khai was among dozens of similar engagements in which I and all Blue Max pilots participated during this period. It was an emotional grind reflective of the physical grind that was taking place on the ground. The ARVN was slogging against the entrenched NVA in a contest of attrition. The good news was that the NVA, mostly because of Allied air superiority, were getting the worst of it in terms of casualties.

The relative stalemate on the ground took on an aspect of constancy in which whatever progress occurred was not, in the day-to-day scheme of things, immediately obvious. In an environment of such a perceived absence of progress, frustration was an ugly result. Typically, that frustration promoted and exacerbated existing doubts and conflicts that existed among us.

The net result of all this was that with little good news, frustration was taking its toll. Along with this, the loss of two crews, combined with the awareness of an unusual number of total aviation losses, wore steadily on the morale in Blue Max and in other aviation units committed to the An Loc battle.

In the environment that had developed during this period, the Blue Max morale was dealt another blow on May 24, when CW2s John Henn and Ike Hosaka were the next victims of an SA-7 missile shoot-down. They were on a Medevac escort mission flying at approximately 4,000 feet near the village of Tan Khai when they were engaged by an NVA SA-7 gunner. As in previous similar incidents, clear descriptions of what happened were difficult to come by. One of the Medevac pilots described flying toward the pickup site when suddenly they saw an explosion near their aircraft where the Blue Max Cobra had been, and then there was nothing. Others in the area reported seeing the tailboom separate from the Cobra, followed by a flat spin descent, ending in an explosion on the ground.

Whatever the details, it was now the third crew and aircraft that Blue Max had lost since the beginning, on April 5, of the Loc Ninh/An Loc battles.

VII
UNTHINKABLE THOUGHTS

Somewhere around the end of May or beginning of June, there was a developing sense that the ARVN were gaining the upper hand, both in An Loc and to the south along Highway 13. Generally, as aviators, we were able to evaluate the progress of the battle in terms of the antiaircraft fire that we received. We had begun to notice that throughout the battle area, we were able to conduct our operations with less harassment by enemy gunners than we'd experienced in the previous months. Nonetheless, we remained respectful of the NVA's great equalizer, the SA-7.

After John Henn and Ike Hosaka were shot down on May 24, there was fairly unanimous and universal acknowledgment from all quarters that they had, indeed, been shot down by a missile. Higher command levels and intelligence didn't attempt to dilute reality with terms like "possible missile." The SA-7 had appeared in other battle areas, notably the Central Highlands around Kontum and Pleiku and in the I Corps area south of the Demilitarized Zone. The enemy had, by now, successfully engaged Air Force FAC (forward air controller) OV-10 Bronco aircraft as well as large C-130 transport aircraft.

This acknowledgment seemed to open the door to discussions about countermeasures and evasion in the missile environment. Unfortunately, few of the countermeasure ideas were feasible for application with our Cobras.

Air Force C-130s and Army CH-47 helicopter crews reported some apparent success in having crew members equipped with flare pistols posted at the doors and windows of their aircraft while flying through areas of likely engagement. The idea was that since the SA-7 was an infrared homing or heat seeking missile, its guidance system could be confused by firing flares from an exposed aircraft, thus providing an alternative, hotter heat source to which the missile would home. There were several reports, mostly unsubstantiated, of success with this method. Success or not, there was little applicability to our Cobras which did not have windows or doors though which a pistol could be fired.

Army command information told us that the missile's guidance system was effective only when the target was significantly above the launcher's horizon. If the target were too low, ground clutter would confuse the missile's infrared sensing, and the gunner would not be able to establish an infrared "lock." The implication of this was that if we were fired upon, then we should attempt to get our Cobra as low as possible. Again, the practicality of this kind of maneuver in evading a missile traveling at Mach 1.5 was a bit dubious.

Probably the most practical advice that we were provided was that aviation units such as ours operating in missile threat environments should have an operating practice in which an agreed-upon signal would be broadcast by anyone in the unit immediately on sighting a missile launch. Such a warning probably wouldn't give us enough of an advance in order to evade the missile, but at least we'd be provided with an idea of what was about to hit us. In Blue Max, we agreed that whenever someone saw a missile launch, that that person would simply broadcast as quickly as possible the words, "Missile, Missile, Missile."

The lack of practical countermeasures to the SA-7 added to the frustration among us. In contrast to our previous experience in which we were accustomed to having a procedure or countermeasure for any possible emergency or threat, we found little comfort in the knowledge that our daily missions exposed us to a threat against which we were virtually defenseless.

With little really useful advice coming from any of our traditional sources about what we could do to increase our safety in the SA-7 environment, we quickly determined that our most reliable information source would be the one that troops in combat have relied upon throughout the history of warfare—each other. Dinner conversation and after hours club conversation invariably included a variety of exchanges of different ideas of responses to the "what ifs" that lurked in the minds of all of us.

In that vein, I remember vividly one conversation that I had with a fellow officer one evening after supper.

In late May and early June, Captain Harry Davis was brand new to

Blue Max. He was a senior captain who had had a prior Vietnam tour as a fixed wing pilot. Time and events would keep us from knowing one another well, but I have never forgotten a conversation that we had one evening as we were relaxing in the shade of the Blue Max operations hooch after supper.

Harry and I were discussing the difficulty of operating in a missile threat environment. I had made a statement to the effect that if one were to take a missile in flight that there was probably nothing one could do. Harry seemed to bristle at my comment. This former fixed wing pilot, brand new to Blue Max, emphatically told me that, regardless of the emergency in which one finds oneself in an aircraft, that one continues to fly the aircraft until one can't. I'd probably heard variants of that statement before but, somehow, Harry's emphasis and conviction in the way he said it at that moment commanded my attention. I felt almost sheepish about what I'd said.

In an attempt to salvage what was left of my pride and to recover from my embarrassment at what I'd said, I managed to shift the conversation. We began to discuss what our actions would be in "continuing to fly the airplane" in the event that one of us found ourself the target of an SA-7. I told Harry that I had recently read a magazine article that told of successful tactics with which Israeli F4 Phantom pilots had evaded Russian built missiles in the Six Day War of 1967. They had had success by turning and diving in the direction of the missile. The idea was to force the missile into a turn with too short a radius to be physically possible to execute and remain on target. The missile would lose its homing lock and fly off harmlessly.

Another benefit of that maneuver was that it would put the heat source —the exhaust stack— on the opposite side of the aircraft. We believed that a missile homing with a direct course into the exhaust stack would result in the missile actually entering the stack with the result that it would detonate inside the helicopter's turbine engine. That scenario would have the probable unhappy result of the entire helicopter exploding in what would surely be an unsurvivable event.

A missile homing toward an exhaust stack from an angle, say greater than 45 , would be less likely to enter the exhaust stack. The most likely result of this scenario would be that the tailboom would be separated from the aircraft as had happened in the cases of the two Blue Max Cobras that had already been lost to SA-7s.

The discussion then turned to how one would control the helicopter after the tailboom had been separated.

The changes in physical and control characteristics of the Cobra following the loss of the tail boom were pretty obvious. There would be an immediate and drastic forward shift of the center of gravity with the nose of the aircraft wanting to tuck forward into a dive. The loss of the tail boom would also include the loss of the tail rotor, the purpose of which is to provide a counterforce to the torque that turns the main rotor when power is applied. Without a tail rotor, there would be no such counterforce, so the fuselage would want to immediately spin to the right. This situation could be addressed by making sure that all power to main rotor was off as in a normal autorotation. [12]

he most essential controls during a tailboom-less descent would be to

---

[12]Autorotation is the means by which a helicopter is landed in a "power off" emergency. In a fixed-wing aircraft, when power is off, the aircraft is controlled aerodynamically to glide to a landing area. In fixed wing, the glide is initiated by keeping a nose low attitude that results in a shallow dive. This assures that the aircraft maintains an airspeed that will allow the airflow over the wings to continue to provide lift to the aircraft. As the aircraft approaches the landing area, it is "flared" by raising the nose to slow the air speed and slow the descent in order to touch down with a slower vertical rate of descent. In order to successfully complete this maneuver in a fixed- wing aircraft, it is necessary to have an extended, flat, open area preferably a runway—in order to accommodate the rollout of the aircraft following touch down. In helicopters, things are quite different. Their flight depends on the main rotor providing lift. This can be done only when the rotor is rotating. When power is lost, the immediate response of the pilot is to remove all power from the rotor system by removing all pitch from the rotor. At the same time, the pilot lowers the nose of the aircraft in order to maintain a specified forward airspeed. The result of these actions is that the aircraft continues to fly forward while entering a high rate of descent. The descent results in air moving upward through the rotor system, causing the rotor to continue to turn, much in the same manner as a child's pinwheel turns in a draft. The pilot then guides the aircraft to a landing area. Upon reaching the landing area, the pilot then flares the aircraft in order to reduce forward airspeed. This maneuver also increases the airflow through the rotor system and tends to increase the rotor speed. The pilot reacts by increasing the rotor pitch which decreases the rate of descent of the aircraft. As the aircraft approaches touch down, the pilot increases the rotor pitch, further reducing the rate of descent to a point that the aircraft is "cushioned" onto the ground. There is typically little or no ground roll when this maneuver is properly executed, so a large open area is not necessary—any flat area that will accommodate a couple of diameters of the plane of the rotor can suffice.

maintain aft cyclic (cyclic corresponds to the yoke or "stick" in a fixed-wing aircraft) to attempt to maintain a level attitude following the forward shift of the center of gravity and to maintain a flat pitch on the rotor in order to maintain rotor speed. We also discussed the idea of firing out the 40-mm grenades and 7.62 ball ammunition from the turret under the nose of the aircraft in order to try to shift the center of gravity rearward.

Unknowingly, Harry and I had just developed the only known emergency procedure for landing a tail-boom-less Cobra following an SA-7 strike. Neither of us really believed it could be done, but it made for good conversation after dinner. I mentally filed what I considered to be the only emergency procedure in existence for surviving an SA-7 strike.

VIII
BREAKOUT FROM AN LOC

As May wound down and June began, the North Vietnamese slowly began to lose their grip on An Loc and Highway 13 to the south. With heavy casualties on both sides the ARVN slowly advanced northward along Highway 13, and the Vietnamese Airborne troops fought their way southward along the highway from An Loc.

By mid-June, the Vietnamese Airborne had advanced to near the hamlet of Tan Khai, approximately 10 kilometers south of An Loc. The advance continued to be a slog, and, even as the Airborne troops continued southward, the NVA continued to make their presence known. It was apparent, though, that the NVA's attempt to take An Loc had failed, and the Vietnamese leadership on both sides understood this. About this time, the Saigon leadership determined that the Vietnamese Airborne would be redeployed to assist in retaking the city of Quang Tri in the northern part of South Vietnam. Quang Tri had endured an attack that was eerily similar to what had occurred at An Loc—with one major difference: Quang Tri was totally in the hands of the North Vietnamese. The South Vietnamese command judged that deployment of their airborne troops to that area would provide the necessary muscle to retake Quang Tri.

The immediate significance of this to Blue Max and other 229th Assault Helicopter Battalion units assigned to Task Force Garry Owen[13] was that the Vietnamese Airborne troops would be extracted from the An Loc/Highway 13 battlefield by Hueys flown by pilots of the 229th Combat Aviation Battalion. These Hueys would be protected by the Cobras of Blue Max.

---

[13]Task Force Garry Owen was what remained in Vietnam in the spring/summer of 1972 of the 1st Cavalry Division (Airmobile). From mid-1971, until early 1972, a single brigade of the 1st Cav had remained in country and was designated 3rd Brigade (separate), 1st Cavalry Division (Airmobile). Early in 1972, ground combat units of the brigade were redeployed the U.S. Remaining elements of the brigade were redesignated as Task Force Garry Owen. Brigadier General Hamlet, previously commanding general of 3rd Brigade (separate) remained as commander of Task Force Garry Owen. As the task force commander was a colonel slot, BG Hamlet was subsequently replaced by COL John Brandenburg.

On June 19, I logged 6.4 hours of flight time in support of the Vietnamese Airborne in their southward advance. Although there was plenty of contact between the Airborne troops and the NVA, there was no noticeable anti-aircraft fire. Most of the day was spent orbiting a short distance away from where the Airborne troops were engaged. I recall engaging one target which was described as a suspected NVA ammunition storage site. At the coordinates that I was given, I could see what looked like a small shed. I engaged it in a steep dive from between 5,000 and 6,000 feet, and my first rounds produced a large secondary explosion. It was a satisfying moment in what was otherwise a tense day of waiting in the air—what we sometimes referred to as "boring holes in the sky." At one point, I decided to see how high I could fly a Cobra. I flew it to 10,000' before I could no longer climb or maintain airspeed. I guess that I was able to check off some kind of bucket list entry with that.

During that day, we learned that an attempt would be made on the following day to extract the Vietnamese Airborne from their Highway 13 positions. A time was set, and a pick-up point was selected. I don't recall the time, but the pickup point was to be in the vicinity of the village of Tan Khai.

The operation would be a debacle.

While the North Vietnamese had clearly been defeated in the An Loc area, their capability to wreak havoc on helicopters had not been eliminated. Shortly after 8:00 a.m. on June 20, a heavy fire team (3 Cobras), along with aviation elements from F Troop, 9th Cavalry arrived in the Tan Khai area to support the planned extraction of the Vietnamese Airborne. At the beginning, two Cobras with crews were lost immediately. The Blue Max bird, crewed by pilot 1st Lieutenant Steven Shields[14] and CPT Ed Northup [15] was shot down by 12.7mm ground fire coming from three directions. Shields and Northup were able to land the aircraft, but they were killed by North Vietnamese small arms fire as they exited their aircraft.

---

[14]In 2011, members of Steve Shields' family traveled to Vietnam in order to place a memorial at the site of Steve's crash.

[15]Ed Northup was a 1969 graduate of West Point.

Almost simultaneously with the shoot-down of Shields and Northup, a Cobra flown by 1LT Louis Breuer and CW2 Burdette Townsend was struck by an SA-7 surface-to-air missile. Witnesses to the shoot-down reported that their helicopter appeared to explode in flight, an
indication that the missile had flown into the exhaust stack on the engine. Also, their bird was reportedly hit at a low altitude, perhaps less than 1,500 feet. If true, that challenged the idea of flight near the horizon as an evasive tactic.

The loss of all of these men was a cruel blow to the units involved. 1LT Breuer had been nicknamed "Animal" by his comrades. He had recently been reassigned to F Troop, 9th Cavalry from the 101st Airborne Division. Two years earlier he had distinguished himself as a star receiver on the Red Raider football team at Texas Tech.

The immediate consensus of all involved was that the North Vietnamese had prepared an anti-aircraft ambush. Realizing that continued helicopter operations at the site would most likely result in further loss of aircraft and crews, the extraction of the Vietnamese Airborne was canceled for that day. Later, it was rescheduled for the following day, June 21st. The pickup point was moved some distance further south on Highway 13.

Disappointment and discouragement are words too soft to describe the emotions of the members of the aviation units involved. This was particularly true in Blue Max where eight of the unit's 32 pilots had now been lost in combat operations. I can't recall a more frustrating time in my two years in Vietnam combat. The question of the ultimate purpose for which these men were sacrificed loomed ever larger in my mind. It was a question that, at the time, seemed to have no satisfactory answers. I had extreme difficulty in reconciling the apparent conflict of, on one hand, executing a strategy of overall withdrawal from the war while, on the other hand, committing ourselves to activities that would surely result in continued people losses. My feelings at the time were very personal, and I doubt that I was able to accurately assess the level of frustration that was present in my Blue Max comrades. In any case, I felt that my inability to reconcile this apparent conflict was such that I could not realistically continue to commit myself to a career in the Army. I decided that I would, at a reasonable time after returning to the U.S., resign my commission. Here, I repeat my previous statement that I find extreme empathy for the current members of our military who find themselves in the position on the "point of the spear" in executing what seems to many to be an irrational strategy in Afghanistan.

IX
MISSILE!MISSILE!MISSILE!

There wasn't much sleep happening during the night of June 20th. Assignments for the following day's activities were made, and I knew that I would be flying as part of a three helicopter heavy fire team providing escort to the Hueys that would be making another attempt to extract the Vietnamese Airborne troops from Highway 13. Our fire team would be led by CW2 Ron Tusi. CPT Harry Davis would be flying as co-pilot/gunner in Ron's front seat. CW3 Russ Toms, a second tour aviator, would be flying the second ship in the flight. His front seat would be WO Ron McCullough, who was a recent arrival in the unit. I would be flying the number three ship with CPT Marco Cordon as my co-pilot gunner. I did not know Marco well, as he was also a recent arrival in Blue Max. I did know that he was a second tour aviator, so I assumed that he would have pretty good air sense.

There was little conversation before the mission. Curiously, what conversation there was included speculation that the NVA probably had few, if any, missiles remaining in their inventory. In retrospect, I have to wonder how we rationalized such speculation against the shoot-down of Breuer and Townsend by an SA-7 on the previous day.

Ron Tusi had a way of instilling confidence. A Warrant Officer, he was one of the finest leaders that I encountered in two years of combat. When he was flying he was in charge. He had no difficulty in instructing senior officers, even including Generals, as to what was expected of them in a variety of situations. He was all business in the air, and his voice on the radio was the epitome of confidence.

Before flying to our forward base at Lai Khe on the morning of the 21st, Ron and Russ and I met to discuss how we would support the troop-carrying Hueys during the extraction. All of us seemed to agree —for some inexplicable reason—that the threat of missiles was probably slight. We decided that keeping two of our Cobras high would provide us with the best observation of the entire area around the extraction point. Ron would fly the low Cobra flying 360° patterns around the Hueys as they approached the pickup zone, picked up their troops, and departed. Russ and I would orbit at altitude, firing rockets into the most likely areas of NVA concentration during the extraction. We discussed the possibility of missiles, and Ron reiterated the only sure response that we had: anyone observing a missile launch would immediately switch his radio to Guard[16] and repeat, "Missile! Missile! Missile!"

My memory of the flight to Lai Khe for forward staging that morning is a fog. I'm sure that all of us were more than a little anxious, given the circumstances of the previous day. While we were convincing ourselves that things would be better that day, we were expecting the worst.

When the time came for the Hueys and us to depart Lai Khe, everything was "go." The weather was good, and there was no known enemy activity at the pickup zone that would preclude the commencement of the operation. We were ready with full fuel and fully armed. We proceeded north several kilometers to the east of Highway 13. My memory is that the Hueys, accompanied by Tusi's Cobra flew north to the area around Chon Thanh at altitude. Shortly after passing Chon Thanh, the flight, less Russ Toms and I, descended to low level to approach the pickup zone.

At the pickup zone, things seemed to proceed rather smoothly. There were reports of sporadic small arms fire, but there were no reports of indirect (artillery or mortar) fire on the landing zone, nor were there reports of heavy anti-aircraft fire. Russ and I remained at altitude— above 4,000 feet. We were in a standard, circular, clockwise orbit east of the highway. When we were flying the part of the orbit that flew from southeast to northwest, we'd fire several rockets across the highway to the west. These rounds were impacting west of the Hueys in an area where there had been reports of small arms fire.

After our first pass, someone spotted mortar rounds landing on the highway near the pickup zone. It would be a matter of a few adjustments before the rounds would be landing in the pickup zone

---

[16]Guard was a radio frequency reserved for emergencies. It was used by all aviation units from all services in Vietnam. All aircraft in Vietnam had a radio that received messages sent on Guard. It was the frequency over which any aviator in a flight emergency would transmit his "Mayday" message. It was also the frequency over which blanket warnings—for such occasions as B-52 strikes—were transmitted.

where the Hueys were picking up their troops. As Marco and I were in our second dive, Marco spotted the tube flashes of the NVA mortars. After I put a few rockets into the general area, we continued our fairly shallow dive in order to descend to an altitude at which Marco could engage the mortar flashes effectively with the 40mm grenade launcher located in the turret under the nose of our Cobra.

The grenade launcher is a weapon that we often used to cover our "break" after a rocket run. The launcher—which we often called a "chunker"--fired 40mm grenades at a rate of 400 rounds per minute. After launch, the rounds, traveling at a slow velocity, would take several seconds to reach the target. It was a good weapon for dispatching rounds that would arrive on a target at about the same moment that our Cobra would be breaking from its run—its most vulnerable, exposed position.

Just before we broke to the right, Marco fired a burst from the chunker along with a burst from our 7.62mm mini-gun. As we were breaking, he could see the explosions as the rounds landed, and he was quite satisfied that his rounds had landed in a pattern that would have had the mortar flashes at its center. In other words, he was pretty sure that the grenades were where they needed to be.

Soon after we had broken to the right and were turning and climbing to the northeast, we heard Ron Tusi shout into the radio, "MISSILE! MISSILE! MISSILE!" I had just checked my instruments, and I knew that I was climbing through 4,200 feet. At the instant that I heard Ron, I turned my head and looked over my left shoulder to see a thick, white, cork-screw rocket signature heading in my direction. What I saw required no analysis; I didn't look around to see if it might be targeted at another aircraft—I knew exactly where it was targeted. It was coming for us.

Ever since the night that Harry Davis and I had had our after dinner conversation about missiles, I'd been mentally rehearsing my missile evasion/emergency procedure. Whether I was ready or not, I was going to be executing it. I began to maneuver my Cobra into a steep, diving left turn in the direction of the missile. I may have accomplished about 3° of bank along with about 3° of left turn when the missile hit.

Actually, the impact of the missile was surprisingly light. I heard it explode, but the resultant shock on the aircraft seemed light. When recording my thoughts more than forty years ago, I speculated that the missile may not, in fact, have actually struck my aircraft before exploding. The missile's warhead may have been detonated by some type of proximity fuse that caused it to explode within a certain distance of my helicopter.

During my initial reaction to the missile, I did not think about anything other than flying the helicopter. As I mentioned, I had already rolled off the throttle and lowered the collective. [17] Immediately as I sensed the helicopter pitch forward, I knew that the tail-boom had been separated from the aircraft. I reacted immediately to the forward pitch by trying to level the aircraft with the cyclic. [18] In attempting to level the aircraft it was necessary to pull the cyclic back nearly against my chest.

At this point, the question of imminent death for Marco and me was not in doubt. There was no reason to believe that our situation could or would conclude favorably. Certainly, there was no history to support such a hope. Nonetheless, I didn't think about it. Neither, at that moment, did I think about my family or God or anything else outside the cockpit. My only thoughts were to execute to the extent possible what I had mentally rehearsed for the past several weeks.

---

[17] A helicopter's "collective" is an abbreviated way of saying Collective Pitch Control. The collective pitch control lever is located to the left of the pilot's seat. Raising the collective increases the pitch of the main rotor blades throughout their circular travel. There is a a twist-grip throttle, very much like the twist-grip throttle on the handlebar of a motorcycle, that is mounted on the end of the collective. This throttle has a mechanical programmed link that increases throttle when the collective is raised and decreases throttle when the collective is lowered. This combination results in more power being transmitted to the main rotor. The increased power results in the helicopter ascending. The opposite is true when the collective is lowered. The pilot can over-ride the throttle's mechanical programming by using the twist-trip throttle.

[18] The cyclic in a helicopter is similar to the "stick" in older fixed wing aircraft. It is extends from the floor in front of the pilot's seat to a position with the top between the pilot's legs. The pilot controls directions—right, left, fore, and aft—by moving the cyclic in whichever of those directions he/she wants to move the aircraft. The cyclic, through a series of hydraulically-assisted mechanical linkages tilts the plane of the rotor—or the rotor disc—in the direction in which the cyclic is moved. Theoretically, when a helicopter is at a hover, the rotor disc is perfectly level, and the cyclic would be perfectly vertical.

After controlling the aircraft to the most level attitude possible, I attempted to broadcast a "Mayday" call. The lack of sound of my helmet earphones made it clear that the aircraft radios were not working—the mayday call went nowhere. I also became aware that I was hearing no radio transmissions from anyone else. Marco and I were in a capsule, completely isolated from the rest of humanity, and descending to what was surely an appointment with our deaths.

Because I'd already bottomed the collective, there was no power or torque being transmitted to the main rotor. As expected, though, the fuselage was spinning slowly about the rotor mast. I say "expected" because there was no tail rotor to counteract the small amount of torque that the up rushing air was imparting to the main rotor. In American built helicopters, the main rotors rotate counter-clockwise about the mast. Anyone with a background in high school physics will know that Isaac Newton's Third Law of Motion posits that "for every action, there is an equal and opposite reaction." In a helicopter, this means that as torque is applied to turn the main rotor, an equal and opposite torque will be applied to the fuselage to which the rotor is connected. Ordinarily, the helicopter's tail rotor provides the force necessary to keep the fuselage from spinning due to this counter-torque. When the tail-boom —upon which the tail rotor is mounted—was severed from our Cobra, there was no way of off-setting the counter-torque applied to our fuselage, so we spun slowly about the main rotor mast.

During our first rotation about the mast, we came face to face with the confirming reality of our situation (the truth is that we really didn't require much confirmation—we were quite aware of our plight). After we had rotated approximately 180°, we were afforded, at our approximate 12 o'clock and slightly below us, a magnificent view of our tail-boom as it tumbled toward Earth. There probably aren't too many experiences more stark than that of observing from one half of your aircraft, the other half, separated and some distance away and hurtling toward a destination different than your own.

One of the mysteries of Marco's and my adventure was that we were able to talk via intercom with one another. Although we'd lost communication via radio with anyone outside our aircraft, our intercom continued to function.

As I continued executing my mentally rehearsed emergency procedure, my next thoughts were to jettison weight from the aircraft. The Cobra that we were flying was armed with two cylindrical rocket pods on each of the wing stores (the stub wings that extend from either side of the fuselage just below the engine compartment), several hundred 40mm grenades, and several thousand rounds of 7.62mm ball ammunition. The grenades and ball ammunition were fired from the nose turret which was controlled by the copilot gunner.

The rocket pods were mounted with electronically activated explosive bolts. I used the electrical switch in an attempt to detonate the explosive bolts and jettison the pods, but there was apparently no electrical signal, and the pods failed to jettison. After that, I attempted to unload the pods by firing out my remaining rockets—there were probably about 30 of an initial load of 76 remaining—but, once again, there seemed to be no electrical signal. I then asked Marco to try to fire out the turret weapons, the 7.62mm mini-gun and the 40mm grenade launcher, but he was unable to do so.

By this time, I'd done most of what I could do...nothing to do now except to try to keep it level and ride it down. The next critical point would be at about tree top level when I would begin to pull up on the collective—in pilot jargon that would be called "pulling pitch." In a normal autorotation this is done to increase the pitch of the blades generating some lift in order to slow, or cushion, the rate of descent. I decided that I would simply pull pitch at the normal altitude. There are no second chances for that maneuver. You pull pitch in order to cushion but the increased bite of the rotor in the air also slows the rotor. If you pull too high, the slowing rotor speed reduces lift, and you land hard. If you pull too low, you hit the ground before the lift can be effective, and you land hard.

There were several times during the descent that I could feel "bumping" in the cyclic. This was accompanied by slight forward pressure on the cyclic. When I felt this bumping, I'd allow the cyclic to ease forward until the bumping stopped. A few years later, in a conversation with Larry McKay, he related to me that Bell Helicopter had done a computer simulation of our descent. Their simulation indicated that if we'd descended from one or two hundred feet higher altitude that we'd have had a main rotor separation due to "mast bumping." I realized hen that the bumping that I was feeling was mast bumping. Mast bumping occurs when the plane of the rotor disc is at such an extreme angle to the mast that the rotor hub strikes the mast upon which it is mounted. The mast, in technical terms, is nothing more than a steel pipe. Mast bumping results in the rotor hub carving a groove in the mast. If the mast bumping is allowed to continue, the groove is cut completely through the mast.

As the descent continued, I glanced at the horizon realizing that this was going to be my last view of Earth. I didn't place any value on it, but my last view was going to be a nondescript, fairly flat jungle, laced with small stream beds leading to the Song Be River a few kilometers to the east. At the same time, I thought briefly of my wife Mary and my daughter Maureen and what might have been.

There wasn't much time for thinking of such things, though. The ground was coming fairly fast, and I needed my concentration for my last control movement—pulling pitch. Marco, who had actually been looking at the instrument panel, recalled in his report that our rate of descent was about 1,500 feet per minute. At that rate, our descent would have been about 2-1/2 minutes.

As the trees began to reach up quickly, I began to pull up on the collective. The fuselage seemed to begin to spin much more violently, but the spin stopped as the helicopter penetrated the crown of what was actually a fairly light forest. Almost at once, I felt the helicopter slam against the trunk of a tree. I continued to pull all of the pitch that was available until I could raise the collective no further. We continued to descend along a tree trunk, striking branches as we fell. Each branch was like a rescuing arm, reaching out to break our rate of fall. Finally, we struck the ground, coming to rest on a large patch of over- mature bamboo that had collapsed to near horizontal providing a large wooden cushion.

We were alive!

X
ON THE GROUND

We were definitely alive, but we definitely weren't out of the woods. Literally or figuratively.

Marco and I were probably thinking the same thing. Both of us knew of too many helicopter crashes that might have been survivable, but the crews had been lost to fire or explosion. I don't recall that either of us spoke as we found ourselves seated in our Cobra on the ground. Each of us moved instantly to exit the aircraft. In Marco's case, he simply opened his front canopy hatch and climbed out normally. In my case, my canopy hatch was jammed, and I could not open it. On discovering this, I immediately took the break-out knife that was mounted in the cockpit and began to chop the canopy plexiglass on the left side of my seat (opposite the movable hatch). I was chopping so intently that when Marco went around the nose of the aircraft to open my hatch, he had to grab my arm to divert my attention to the fact that the hatch was open. The open hatch allowed my hasty exit. In my haste to leave the aircraft, I didn't think to shut down the engine. The engine was still running at idle as it had been throughout our descent.

During his exit, Marco noted that the impact of our landing had forced several of the 2.75" rockets out of the pods on the wing stores. They were scattered about in front of our helicopter. He also noticed that the Cobra's skids had spread noticeably as a result of the impact. Although neither of us had suffered any immediately detectable trauma, it was clear that our landing had not been altogether soft.

As we moved to get quickly away from the aircraft, we saw that we were in a small clearing. Our Cobra was on one edge of the clearing. We ran to a tree line on the opposite side of the clearing in a bid to conceal ourselves. We knew that we had landed in an area where there were no friendly forces present. What we didn't know was whether there were any enemy in our immediate area. The possibility of that became apparent when, as we reached the tree line, we found empty C-ration cans similar to those issued by the U.S. Army—except that these cans were a lighter shade of olive drab than we were accustomed to seeing, and they had Chinese markings on them. We didn't check to see if any of them had contained fruit cocktail or date pudding.

Further evidence of enemy presence showed itself as we entered the tree line. Immediately in front of us, a few meters back in the trees, was a huge NVA bunker. It was probably much smaller than I perceived it, but it was more than a little intimidating. During my first tour in Vietnam, I'd spent most of my time as a Artillery Forward Observer with an Infantry Rifle Company. In that role I'd been in many enemy base camps and had seen many bunkers. This bunker was as well constructed as any I'd ever seen. The overhead cover was supported by freshly-cut logs about 4" in diameter, and it had at least 12" of earth over that. I don't recall seeing other bunkers nearby, but this bunker was clearly larger than would have been required for an observation post or listening post. It was large enough to house at least 4 or 5 North Vietnamese. The freshly cut logs and the C-ration cans told us that if the enemy weren't here, they'd been there recently. Since we'd run virtually straight toward the bunker and weren't shot at, we were able to judge that, for the moment, we'd happened by when no one was home. We were clearly in an enemy base of some sort.

Both of us had left our flight helmets in the helicopter. I was wearing my survival vest, and both of us had our 38-caliber revolvers. That was the total of the equipment that we had with us.

As we settled into our spot, Marco extended his hand to me in congratulations. We mutually inquired as to our condition and determined that we were both OK.

The survival vest was, in most respects, a pretty practical piece of equipment. It contained several items that one might find useful. Some that immediately come to mind are minor first aid items, pain pills, waterproof matches, a large silk "blood-chit" with a U.S. flag and distress messages written in common Asian languages, and an emergency survival radio. There was even, curiously enough, a condom. Most items were pretty self-explanatory, but I never did manage to visualize the circumstances under which a downed pilot was going to find a need for such an item. Maybe someone was confused about the meaning of the words survival and emergency.

The item of interest to me at the moment was the survival radio. I wanted to notify our comrades that we were OK and to try to coordinate some kind of rescue plan. Unfortunately, the radio did not work. I don't recall whether I threw it at a tree or returned it to the survival vest.

Neither of us doubted that there would be an immediate search to locate us. We had total confidence that our comrades and others were going to do everything possible to remove us safely from the jungle. Nonetheless, I began to think about the possibility of having to leave the area where we were. If that had been necessary—we didn't know if or when the bad guys would be coming back for dinner—it would have to have been an escape and evasion ype activity. Without a functioning radio we would have no way of coordinating our movement with friendly forces. I knew that the bad guys were most likely to be to our west, near the highway. Moving in that direction would not have been my choice. I knew that the Song Be River was a few kilometers to our east, and my thoughts were that we would move toward the river and follow it south. There were several towns along the river, and, to the best of my knowledge, they were all in friendly hands. Phuoc Vinh, which had an ARVN facility, would have been the nearest large town in that direction.

Fortunately, all of this was but a fleeting thought, as we very soon heard the sound of Cobras flying at low level and obviously flying in a search pattern. When we judged that they were about to overfly our position, we ran into the open area to our front and began waving our arms. On the second pass, I recognized Ron Tusi in the back seat of one of the Cobras, and he gave us a "thumbs up" signal. We knew we'd been located. The Cobras left the mmediate area, and we returned to the tree line.

Ron and Harry Davis, his co-pilot gunner, had watched the entire shoot-down from the launch of the missile to the point at which our Cobra disappeared below the treetops. They were able to move quickly to the location where we landed.

Another person, Major Ernie Isbell, had also witnessed the entire event. Ernie was leading the flight of five Hueys, called "Black Flight," which we had been escorting. His flight was touching down as the missile was fired.

WO Bill Wright, whose call-sign was Black Five, heard Ron Tusi's call, "Missile! Missile! Missile!" just as he was about to touch down as the last Huey in Black Flight. He did not see the missile launch, but he looked up as Marco and I were, as he put it, "fluttering down" through about 2000 feet. He didn't see the tail-boom. He thought that he had a good fix on the spot where we had gone down, and he asked for and received permission from Black Lead, Ernie Isbell, to break off from Black Flight and proceed to our location. About the same time, Ron Tusi and Harry Davis had confirmed that Marco and I were OK, so Wright knew that a rescue attempt was likely.

WO Wright and his copilot flew as quickly as possible to our location. Before leaving the pickup zone, they had picked up four Vietnamese Airborne troops along with their gear. They also loaded the bodies of five deceased Airborne troops. In effect, this meant that, including the crew of four, there were already 13 people on board their Huey when they began to search for Marco and me. Given the typically high density altitude[19] of a June mid- afternoon in South Vietnam, it is likely that the density altitude at sea level at the time of the search and rescue would have been on the order of 5,000' or 6,000' or even higher. Such a density altitude would significantly impair the capability of an already fully-loaded Huey. Wright and his copilot would need to draw on the full measure of their piloting skills in order to hover their helicopter in such adverse conditions. Addition of two more passengers would only tax them and their helicopter further.

Black 5's concerns weren't limited to helicopter performance. While

---

[19]Density Altitude applies a temperature factor to the actual altitude at a location. Higher temperatures result in lower air density. Density also decreases as altitude increases. Higher than "standard" temperature will reduce air density so that the density of air at sea level will match the density, at standard temperature, of air at a higher altitude. Aircraft performance at sea level will replicate that at a higher altitude in higher density altitude conditions. In South Vietnam temperatures of 110F are not uncommon on June afternoons. Such a temperature can result the performance of an aircraft at sea level matching that of an aircraft at more than 5,000 feet at standard temperature.

enroute to our location he and his crew spotted a group, which they estimated at platoon-sized, of North Vietnamese soldiers moving quickly toward our location. Wright recalls that those troops were no more than 200-300 meters from our position. He and his copilot knew that they wouldn't have much time.

While WO Wright, with the assistance of directions from CW2 Tusi, flew to our location, Marco and I continued to lay low in the tree-line at the edge of the small open area. As we observed the approach of Wright's aircraft, it quickly became clear that the rotor disc of his Huey was larger than any area near us that was free of trees. There was no spot where the Huey could be landed. I was optimistic, though, that if Wright and King could hover their bird low enough, Marco and I might be able to jump up and grab the skids.

WO Wright and and his copilot made several attempts to do just that, but each time that they tried to hover down, their main rotor would strike trees, and they were forced to pull back up again.

Mindful of the approaching NVA, Wright had directed his copilot to stay on the Huey's controls with him. He felt that there was a very real possibility that one of them would be shot, and It was a precaution taken against that possibility—the other pilot would be able to continue to fly the aircraft without a transfer of control.

As Wright and his copilot continued with their heroics, someone in their helicopter, apparently inadvertently, stepped on one of the floor switches in the cargo bay that is used to "key" the helicopter's radio transmitter, causing what is known as a "hot mike." The sounds from their helicopter, including the sound of trees being chopped by rotor blades, were transmitted to all of the other aircraft in the area. The sound contributed an audio track to what was already a high and intense drama.

While Wright and his crew continued to try to find some way to to bring their helicopter to an altitude low enough that Marco and I would have a chance at jumping to grab one of the Huey's skids, I felt a developing sense that the natural barriers formed by the trees would ultimately prevent the success of such an idea. About then, while looking at the altitude of the Huey and at the wreckage of our Cobra,

69

I thought that there might be a possibility that if the Huey could be hovered directly over our Cobra, Marco and I could climb to the top of our wreckage, then we might be able to jump from there to the the Huey's skid. Marco and I discussed the idea and, once again, ran into the clearing where I climbed to the top of the main rotor pylon of the Cobra. I was able to get enough stable footing to be able to jump toward the Huey's skid. WO Wright once again lowered his bird; I jumped and grabbed a skid. At the same time, the Crew Chief, SP5 David Vaughn, kneeling in the doorway, reached down to grab me and pulled me into the Huey. Marco would then repeat the same process.

It wasn't that easy. Marco, in addition to being several inches shorter than I, had been injured. He hadn't—possibly due to the effects of adrenalin rush—realized this while we were on the ground. He would later learn that the impact of our crash had left him with three compression fractures of spinal vertebrae. Jumping to a moving helicopter skid from a narrow surface on top of a downed helicopter was no simple or painless task .

One of the Vietnamese Airborne troops inside the helicopter smiled and graciously offered me his web seat. I accepted. About then I noticed the five corpses wrapped in ponchos and lying on the floor. Apparently these fallen Airborne heroes had not died that morning. The odor from the corpses was overwhelming. The air currents around the hovering helicopter were directed in such a way as to assure that there was no air flow flushing through the helicopter's passenger bay.

After what seemed a long time, but I'm sure wasn't more than four or five minutes, the Huey crew was able to assist Marco aboard, and our probably overloaded Huey was off to our forward base at Lai Khe.

While we were still on the ground and I was weighing the possibility that we might not be able to mount WO Wright's Huey, I later—many years later—learned that someone else was considering the same thought. CW2 Ron Tusi, while continuing to orbit Black Five and provide aerial security, also weighed that possibility. He developed another rescue plan which had him landing his Cobra at a clearing a short distance away and coming to get Marco and me. He would then take us back to his Cobra and fly us out.

WO Bill Wright chops tree branches with his rotor blades while hovering over our downed Cobra. SP5 Dave Vaughn reaches down to assist my entry while Marco watches from the Cobra wing.
(Artistic depiction by my brother, Jim Tibbs)

The Cobra has no provision for passengers beyond the pilot and co-pilot. A procedure for rescue has been devised, however, and Ron began to follow that procedure. He would jettison all four of the cylindrical rocket pods from his Cobra's stub wings. This would allow opening the ammunition bay doors located on the lower fuselage just aft of the nose turret on either side of the aircraft. These doors, hinged at the bottom, were retained by a cable which prevented them being opened beyond horizontal. One person would be placed on each of the lowered doors, and they would each reach through the ammunition bay in order to clasp one anothers' arms.

Ron had successfully jettisoned his rocket pods, and he had landed his Cobra. He and his co-pilot/gunner, CPT Harry Davis, were enroute on foot toward our location when WO Wright's Huey departed. Ron and Harry then knew that we had been rescued and returned to their Cobra, took off, and returned to Lai Khe. As I mentioned, I did not learn of their effort until many years later. Like Marco and me, Ron and Harry were, at that time unaware of the NVA platoon that had been closing on our position.

As WO Wright and his crew flew Marco and me toward Lai Khe, the odor of the bodies in the helicopter continued to overwhelm. I recall that when we passed the town of Chon Thanh enroute, I was tempted to ask our pilots if they could drop us there. Neither Marco nor I had kept our flight helmets when we left our Cobra, so we were unable to use the Huey's intercom or radios. Because we had no ear protection, we couldn't talk over the helicopter noise. Our conversation was limited to a few yelled single words and body language.

A few minutes before Lai Khe came into sight, WO Wright in the pilot's seat of the Huey turned around and asked if either of us would need medical attention. My immediate thought was, "I have a story to tell; I don't need to see a doctor!" Marco, however, said—I thought with some hesitation—that he was feeling a pain in his back and that he felt that he should see a doctor.

We were soon on the ground in Lai Khe. Bill Wright remembers that as soon as his skids touched the PSP (Perforated Steel Plate) of the Lai Khe runway, I immediately jumped out the right side door, ran to the nose of the Huey, kissed it, and ran to his pilot's door and grabbed his hand and shook it. I'm sure that Bill remembers it accurately. Forty-some years later, I don't remember it at all.

From the time that I left Wright's helicopter at Lai Khe, I never saw him or his crew again. Forty years later, he and I connected by telephone, when he, while anticipating his first-ever attendance at a convention of the national Vietnam Helicopter Pilots' Association, decided, on Sunday afternoon, July 8, 2012, to call me on my cell phone. It was the first conversation in the intervening years that either Marco or I had ever had with a member of the crew that rescued us. It was, after all those years, a pleasure to finally be able to express my thanks to him.

Marco would also leave Wright's helicopter at Lai Khe. He boarded another helicopter which transported him to an evacuation hospital in Saigon. There, he would learn the extent of his injuries. He was immediately evacuated to a medical facility in Japan enroute to the United States. As I wrote earlier, our parting on the runway at Lai Khe was the last time that Marco and I would talk or have any knowledge of one another for the next twenty-four years.

Bill Wright remained with his helicopter on the runway at Lai Khe. After shutting down, he proceeded, with his commanding officer, Major Ernie Isbell, to inspect the damage to his Huey after he had used his blade to literally clear his own landing zone to rescue Marco and me. The damage was considerable. The rotor blade was on the verge of breaking into pieces. Major Isbell ordered that the helicopter not be moved until it could be fitted with a new main rotor. It was repaired in place on the runway.

That night, Major Isbell related in a conversation with LTC Lew McConnell, 229th Assault Helicopter Battalion Commander that WO Wright and his copilot had sheepishly and apologetically inquired as to whether they would be incurring any financial liability for intentional damage to a U.S. Army helicopter. Instead, Isbell wrote recommendations for Silver Stars for each of them. The recommendations were subsequently downgraded to Distinguished Flying Crosses. I'm sure that Marco would agree with me that an award of the Silver Star was fully justified.

I know that as a principal who was rescued my judgment may be biased, but the courage and determination displayed by WO Wright and his co-pilot ranks among the most courageous and selfless acts which I witnessed during my Vietnam tours. Marco and I are ery much in their debt. That debt extends to their crew as well. At this point, we have learned that the Crew Chief on the rescue helicopter was David Vaughn of Midland, Michigan. We still have not determined the name of the co-pilot or the door gunner that were in Bill Wright's crew that day. Perhaps, one day, additional fortune will shine upon us and they or a friend will read this account and be prompted to notify us.

XI
HOLDING COURT IN LAI KHE

As WO1 Wright began his long approach to the PSP[20] runway at Lai khe, I could see a jeep with a couple of people standing next to it awaiting our approach. When we landed, one of the men moved to our helicopter to meet us. It was Brigadier General Hamlet who was the commander of Task Force Garry Owen, the remaining elements of 3rd Brigade, 1st Cavalry Division. BG Hamlet didn't appear to betray any emotion. He simply looked at me and said, "Brown, how in the hell did you do that?" As I hesitated momentarily before starting to explain, he might have thought better of asking such a question, and he immediately told me that I should prepare a full written report detailing what we had done. Clearly, BG Hamlet had been as frustrated as anyone at the toll that the SA-7 armed North Vietnamese had been exacting on our pilots.

Almost immediately, another jeep arrived. I don't remember who it was or who sent it, but it was clearly there to pick me up. BG Hamlet asked me what I'd like to do, and I didn't hesitate to respond that I'd like to go to the officers' club. He released me immediately. I sort of levitated into the jeep, and next found myself in a crowded bar room at the Lai Khe officers' club.

I will return to BG Hamlet later in my account, but I would, at this point, like to share a vignette about Hamlet that Marco Cordon shared with me recently.

Marco relates that earlier during the Battle of An Loc that he had been flying a particularly rigorous routine of flights between Lai Khe and An Loc. On one of many occasions, Marco and whoever his aircraft commander was that day had returned to Lai Khe to refuel and rearm. After the aircraft commander had hovered their Cobra to the refuel point, Marco jumped out and began to refuel the aircraft. While he was doing this, a jeep appeared on the other side of the aircraft.

---

[20]PSP refers to Perforated Steel Plate. Originally it was used in World War II for quickly installing temporary runways on islands in the South Pacific. The plates are approximately 5' long by 15" wide. They are formed with linking tabs in order to be fit together to provide a continuous surface on the ground. The perforation in the plate is a pattern of holes of approximately 3" in diameter.

A black fellow got out of the jeep and walked over to the stack of 2.75" rockets and began to position several for rearming. After Marco finished refueling the aircraft, he proceeded to the other side of the aircraft to begin rearming it. As he loaded the first few rockets he noticed that the guy in a t-shirt who was handing him rockets looked familiar—it was BG Hamlet! Important people doing little things for people make lasting impressions!

When I arrived at the officers' club, I found it fairly crowded, mostly with people that I didn't know. It was late afternoon, and most people that I knew were either flying or supporting An Loc operations in some way. Nonetheless, as the story of my shoot-down began to spread, I found that I was in no need of beer money. Occasionally, someone that I knew would come by and we'd talk, but mostly it was chatting and drinking beer with people that I knew only vaguely.

After I'd been there about an hour, I was told that a reporter from the Stars & Stripes wanted to talk with me. I was somewhat surprised, given the uniqueness of what I'd just done, that the only reporter that I ever talked with about the shoot-down was Specialist 4 Jim Smith of the *Stars & Stripes*. His article is copied in the appendices.

After several beers, someone from Blue Max came to pick me up. The unit's Huey command and control helicopter was at the Lai Khe runway. For reasons that I don't recall, there was only one pilot with the bird. "No problem," I think I said as I climbed into the aircraft commander's seat in the Huey. Somehow, I was able to take off and navigate my way back to the Blue Max base at Long Thanh Army Airfield approximately 30 miles from Lai Khe. It was the one and only time that I ever flew so soon after consuming adult beverages. I do not recommend it.

At Long Thanh, it was definitely party night. Blue Max had come through a lot, and my good fortune was clearly a lift for everyone. Our unit club was crowded and joyous that night. That's about as much detail as I can remember.

XII
THE MORNING AFTER

On the morning of June 22, I awakened suddenly. I knew that I would not be flying that day, so I had set no alarm; I intended to sleep in. In the end, I hadn't really imbibed heavily the night before, so I wasn't expecting to be hung over. In retrospect, I don't think that when I went to bed, I realized how much of a toll that the afternoon and evening had taken from me. In any case, it was one of those nights when one awakens abruptly in the morning with no awareness that hours have passed since retiring the previous evening. I lay there in my hooch thinking of the events of the previous day. Given the events of the day, I wondered if I hadn't awakened to some kind of surreal out-of-body experience. That I was somehow alive seemed to require some kind of validation.

Validation came quickly. I pulled back the sheets, and I began to sit up and swing my legs to the floor. OUCH! Every part of my muscular-skeletal system was in pain. It reminded me of an old Shelley Berman routine that I'd heard years earlier in which he was recounting a particularly painful hangover experience (except I knew I didn't have a hangover). He said, "I woke up, and my hair hurt!"

It wasn't my hair, but if I had a single cubic centimeter of tissue that didn't hurt, it was doing a super job of hiding itself. The pain was an intense form of the kind of pain that I used to have after the first or second day of football practice. Every joint was stiff, and any movement was instantly halted as it was swallowed by pain.

It took me three or four attempts at moving to get myself to a point where I could sit on the edge of the bed with my feet on the floor. I was starting to believe I was alive—that this really wasn't some kind of ethereal after-life experience. I wondered whether I might not have suffered some kind of invisible trauma that might account for the way I felt. I checked myself as thoroughly as I could, and I could find nothing that hinted of injury.

There was nothing pressing me. I knew that people were probably going to allow me some time to myself. Most of my fellow pilots would likely be on missions, and there probably wasn't much going on around the unit area. I figured that I'd rest for a bit and then see if I could muster the energy and will to get dressed and walk to the mess hall for whatever might be left of breakfast.

I thought about BG Hamlet's instruction to write a report about what I'd done in the crash. It seemed a daunting task. Where would I start? What was important? How long should it be? How much time should I spend on it?

While sitting there, I happened to glance at a new cassette recorder that I'd recently purchased at the PX. It was pretty state-of-the-art for the times. It was stereo with a couple of speakers and combined a radio and cassette player. It was equipped with two microphones to allow stereo recording. I thought, "Why don't I just voice record my report?" There was no one there to advise me whether it was a bad idea or a good idea.

I began, "On June 21, 1972, I was working on a mission....." I described sequentially what had happened. Occasionally, I'd digress from the sequential flow to provide a parenthetical description of some point that I thought was important at the time. In the end, I probably recorded for about an hour. I'd never heard of a formal military report being provided on audio tape. It seemed so efficient, and I felt that listeners would be able to grasp what I had to say much more effectively if they heard it simply as a conversation. I was feeling a sense of mission about providing something that would really help to save lives. I wanted other pilots to hear what I had to say in a way that a written document couldn't provide. I believed that my audience was my fellow pilots, not BG Hamlet. I felt that it was important to get something to pilots immediately, and if BG Hamlet still needed a written document, I could provide that later.

After it was completed, I listened to the entire tape. It wasn't perfect, but I felt that it was complete, and it communicated what I wanted to say. I put the cassette in its container and sealed it. I wrote the address of BG Hamlet on it. Later, I handed it to a courier who I knew would be going to Bien Hoa where BG Hamlet's office was located.

After I dispatched the tape, I didn't hear about it for several days. After I asked about it repeatedly, someone made a copy of it and returned the original to me. I still have the original with its label, "Cpt Brown's Statement." A transcription of the tape, written by Mike Sloniker, is found in the Appendix.

Gradually, I was able to become mobile, although it was painful. The pain would remain with me for the remainder of the day and for several days afterward. I've never been able to establish the reason for my stiffness and soreness, but I have heard others, when recalling aviation accidents and vehicular crashes, describe the same thing. I don't understand the physiology of it, but apparently it has something to do with an adrenaline rush that accompanies the threat of trauma.

During the day, I received several messages, both congratulating me and informing me of changes resulting from my accident.

Probably of most immediate import was that I was informed that should I wish to consider an option of not flying for the remainder of my tour—which was scheduled to end in October— my wishes would be respected. I appreciated that offer. It was offered in a spirit that understood that I had escaped the Grim Reaper's best shot and that it would be beyond reason to expect me to submit myself to a repeat performance. I agreed with that logic, but I did qualify it to say that I would be amenable to flying non-combat missions. In essence, my flying days in Vietnam were over. I believe that the source of that offer was Gen. Creighton Abrams who was then the MACV (Military Assistance Command Vietnam) commander.

Gen. Abrams also communicated his personal permission for me to be allowed a two week leave in the U.S. I deferred on that; my high school class (Sandpoint [Idaho] High School 1962) would be having its ten-year reunion in August, and I felt that I'd rather postpone the leave in order to coincide with the reunion.

Also on that day, Larry McKay, who had recently relinquished his command of Blue Max to become Task Force Aviation Officer at Task Force Garry Owen, informed me that Blue Max was being withdrawn from the An Loc battle. There was agreement that that battle had been won, and Blue Max would be needed elsewhere in Vietnam.

Elsewhere was the city of Quang Tri in the northern part of South Vietnam. The South Vietnamese military had been driven from that city in April, and they were positioned to mount a counter-offensive to retake the city. Blue Max would be supporting that effort.

I had twice previously been the officer in charge of moving Blue Max between bases in the Bien Hoa-Long Binh area, and those movements had gone well. The impending move would move the unit from its base at Long Thanh Army Airfield in III Corps in southern South Vietnam to Danang Air Base in I Corps in northern South Vietnam. The move would be done using U.S. Air Force transport. I would be responsible for overall coordination and management of the move. The move would involve Army and Air Force assets which would be supplemented by Vietnamese civilian contractors. All of this was pretty straightforward. Just to make it challenging, though, was the requirement that the move be completed within a week.

Moving an aviation unit with all its people, their personal property and equipment, and all the administration and equipment support for a unit on short notice is no small undertaking. It would require much communication and coordination with everyone involved. I was provided with one assistant for the mission. CW2 Tony White had been recovering from a broken leg, and he was conveniently available to assist me. We were able to complete the mission smoothly within the time allowed. Blue Max was accepting missions from Danang within a week.

After the Blue Max had left for Danang and Tony and I became the only occupants of the battery area at Long Thanh came one of the saddest events that occurred during my second tour. While Tony and I were cleaning up our base area, we received word that a CH-47 Chinook helicopter carrying approximately thirty American soldiers to in-country R&R (Rest and Recuperation) in Vung Tau had crashed near our base at Long Thanh. Apparently, one of the rotor blades had separated from a rotor hub at 3000 feet. The helicopter disintegrated at altitude with major parts of it crashing and burning. There were no survivors. Neither Tony nor I chose to become witnesses to the aftermath. To this day, I'm reminded of that every time I hear of a Chinook crash. There have been at least two such crashes—both involving enemy fire—in Afghanistan.

Tony and I stayed a few days after the completion of the Blue Max move in order to turn in or dispose of all the installation property that was left at Long Thanh. As one might expect, that was a tedious process.

After clearing Long Thanh, Tony returned to Blue Max in Danang. I relocated to a hooch at Lassiter Army Heliport at Bien Hoa airbase. Larry McKay had established a temporary job for me there working on aviation matters with Task Force Garry Owen. I remained there for approximately three weeks while awaiting my departure on leave to attend my August class reunion. I honestly don't recall doing much of consequence there, but I was glad to have the time with Larry. We had much to talk about.

XIII
STATESIDE LEAVE AND END OF TOUR

My flight to the U.S. would be on a Boeing 747. They were quite new at the time, and I looked forward to the adventure. The flight would depart from Tan Son Nhut Airport in Saigon. Although I'd done extensive patrolling around the outskirts of Saigon in the aftermath of the 1968 Tet Offensive, I'd never spent any time in the city. In the hope that I might be able to see some of the city, I left a couple of days early to stay at a BOQ (Bachelor Officers' Quarters) at the MACV compound next to Tan Son Nhut.

MACV was a surprise to me. The main building seemed to me like a stateside corporate office building, built of concrete, steel, and glass. There was an officers' club that seemed similar to those that I'd patronized in the states. I learned that I would not be able to freely wander to and from the city, so I settled into a rather boring couple of days at what was known as Camp Alpha. I could walk from there to MACV. I had my first ever Mongolian Barbecue at the MACV officers' club. For a kid from northern Idaho, that was pretty adventuresome exotica.

The time for my flight arrived, and I was off to Travis Air Force Base and then to Spokane, Washington where Mary would meet me. Mary and I had talked once on the MARS [21] since my shoot-down. She had only sketchy information about what had happened. I don't think that I was ever able to fully explain to her what had occurred. Years later, when we first saw Joe Kline's very accurate painting, "Missile! Missile!Missile!" I think that she—and others—were able to understand more clearly what had happened.

By the time that we arrived in Sandpoint, Idaho, our hometown, there

---

[21]MARS is Military Affiliated Radio System. At major U.S. bases, commands would install a shortwave radio station. Its primary use was to connect to amateur shortwave radio hobbyists in the U.S. They would then patch their radios into the telephone system and call collect to telephone numbers provided by the overseas service man. Overseas servicemen were then able to talk via telephone with their loved ones. Calls were limited to five minutes and strict radiotelephone protocols were required.

was general awareness among friends of what had happened. I was able to share my story with my genuinely interested classmates at the class reunion. I even received the prize for the alumnus who had traveled the longest distance to attend the reunion.

The leave time was a blur. Mary and I talked a lot about what would be next. We were committed to my leaving the Army, and we discussed much about how and when we would do that. While home, it occurred to me that upon returning to Vietnam that I would have only two weeks remaining in my tour. To me it didn't make a lot of sense for me to return to Vietnam with such a short time remaining, particularly in view of the fact that I wouldn't be doing any combat flying. I called my Field Artillery branch assignments officer in the Pentagon to share my concerns with him. He agreed that it didn't make a lot of sense but that with all the other personnel turbulence occurring because of the rapid return of Vietnam people, it would simply be more than the system could bear to try to change my assignment to remain in the states.

Following my two week leave, I returned to Vietnam. I returned to Blue Max at Danang where I would stay for the next two weeks. The North Vietnamese fired rockets into the massive base there every single day that I was there. On several occasions their rockets hit barracks buildings, and several soldiers were killed.

I had no duties while in Danang. I spent several days on the beach at the famed China Beach. It wasn't like on TV. The sun rose in the east and set in the west and there were NO women....just a bunch of guys staring at the water and eating shrimp and steak at the Philco- Ford Club. One night I went with several of my comrades to a Korean restaurant and continued my forays into exotic eating. I introduced myself to Bul Go Ki. It was delicious. The next morning, the restaurant was destroyed by an incoming North Vietnamese rocket. I learned that that was the third time that the Korean restaurant had been similarly destroyed. Apparently, the North Vietnamese had a low opinion of the Kim Chee.

During my stay in Danang, Blue Max received orders to stand down. The unit would be deactivated in September. My departure from Vietnam would occur before the stand down. As part of the stand-down the unit's Cobras would have to be flown to Saigon in order to be shipped back to the U.S. I volunteered myself to fly one of the Cobras to Saigon. I'd then have to spend a couple of more days in the Saigon area before once again getting aboard a 747 for my permanent return to the U.S.

The ferry flight was interesting. I was able to fly virtually the entire coastline of South Vietnam from Danang to Saigon. Near Qui Nhon and Nha Trang I saw some of the most beautiful beaches that I've ever seen anywhere. Near Quang Ngai, several U.S. warships were a few miles off-shore. They were providing naval gunfire support to Vietnamese troops a short distance inland. Just as we flew between the ships and the shoreline, we were able to see smoke from their guns. The pucker factor definitely increased, but we passed through the area without incident. It did, however, recall my experience at An Loc with the AC-130 Spectre gunship.

XIV
FORT BENNING

For the second time in three weeks, I was returning to the U.S. in September 1972. After several telephone conversations with Field Artillery Officer Assignments in the Pentagon, I was able to secure an assignment to Fort Benning. It was a long way from Idaho, so Mary and I decided to make a bit of a sight-seeing road trip of it. Part of our trip would take us to Detroit, Michigan, where Mary's older brother would be getting married late in the month. From there, we traveled across southern Ontario, returning to the U.S. at Niagra Falls. It was an amazing time for our nearly three-year old daughter Maureen. We spent several enjoyable days crossing upstate New York, and we spent part of a day at West Point. Then we went on to New York City where we treated Maureen to her first subway ride. She didn't like it. Mary and I softened some of our accumulated stress with a visit to the Rainbow Room in the RCA Building. From there, it was on to Washington, D.C. where we spent a couple of days visiting friends. Fort Benning would be our next, and last, stop on what was a very pleasant trip.

I was assigned to the 121st Aviation Company based at Fort Benning's Lawson Army Airfield. The 121st was a mixed aviation company having three platoons of Hueys and one platoon of Cobras. It was the primary aviation support for the Infantry School headquartered at Fort Benning. I was assigned as the Operations Officer. Infantry School support generated an activity level nearly equal to what I'd seen in combat. Infantry officer basic and advanced courses were constantly cycling through, and they required helicopter support for their intense training activities. The Cobras were kept busy providing support for fire support demonstrations for the various groups of trainees and VIPs as they passed through Fort Benning. Our company also provided Ranger School support at its Dahlonega, Georgia and Eglin Air Force Base Ranger Camps. It was not going to be an assignment for rest and recuperation. I did have good, competent assistants, though, and through division and delegation, we were able to maintain individual work loads at a reasonable level.

One of the more sensitive aspects of my job at Fort Benning was that the 121st Aviation Company was the aviation support for the Army's Southeastern United States Ready Reaction Force. In the late 1960s and early 1970s, stateside Army units were shouldering a significant burden involving riot control. Indeed, the 121st spent much of the month of August 1972 in the Miami/Miami Beach area during the Republican national convention. The RRF portion of our mission also occasioned another unusual assignment. Key Biscayne, Florida was in our area of interest, and every time that President Nixon would visit there, which was quite often, we were required to maintain a number of aircraft and crews on a high alert status. Alert crews were required to remain on post and be available by telephone at all times. The fact that opportunities to visit the Gulf Coast with family were quite restricted was only partially off-set by occasional reconnaissance trips to the Miami/Key Biscayne area.

During my time with the 121st, I did occasional flying. Mostly, I flew Cobras doing firepower demonstrations for Infantry School students and occasional VIPs. I found that I really hadn't recovered emotionally from my shoot-down at An Loc, and I was quite guarded about my approach to flying. Nonetheless, I tried to provide a good show of all the kinds of things that I'd done with the Cobra in combat. It never really became fun, though.

One of the more puzzling aspects to my entry to Fort Benning was that no one there had heard of my shoot-down. Even more puzzling was that no one seemed to have heard anything of An Loc. When I mentioned anything about the experience of flying Cobras in a missile environment, disbelieving stares typified the responses. It seemed to me an enormous disconnect that Army Aviation had played such a key role in what was regarded as the biggest battle of the Vietnam War, and aviators in the U.S. seemed to be so unaware.

his disconnect was even more apparent to me when, about a week after my arrival, I was notified that all of the aviators assigned to 121st Aviation Company were to be scheduled to attend a one hour presentation at Infantry Hall. The subject of the presentation was to be the SA-7 surface-to-air missile. For virtually all of the aviators, it was the first information that they would hear about the missile. At the appointed time, I left my office at Lawson Field and went to Infantry Hall. I was turned away at the door. It seems that, owing to my recent arrival, my security clearance had not yet been validated locally, and the presentation would be classified. I understood this, but, nonetheless, the incongruity of having the only pilot in the Army who had ever survived an SA-7 missile strike being denied entry to a briefing on said missile left me more than a little puzzled.

As weeks passed, my story became more known in the unit. The Company Commander, Major Joffre Filion, took a particular interest in it. He seemed to be very surprised to learn that I had received no decorations or awards as a result of the shoot-down. He led an effort to have me awarded the Army Aviation Association's "Broken Wing Award." The award has a very high bar, and it requires a number of eyewitness statements. I felt quite honored and humbled by the effort that Major Filion made in securing the award. I was also honored to have included among the eyewitness statements, one by Ron Tusi. The clear regard coming from such an esteemed professional was truly an honor for me.

Adding to the honor was that, by sheer coincidence, shortly after the award was approved, it was learned that Brigadier General Hamlet would be visiting Fort Benning. On being notified of my award, he graciously agreed to present it to me.

By the time that BG Hamlet arrived, it was generally known that I had resigned my commission and that I would be leaving the Army soon (June 30, 1973). After presenting me with the award, BG Hamlet expressed regret that I was leaving, but he said he very much understood my reasons. I was extremely grateful to hear such remarks from a man whom I'd come to respect and admire so much.

On June 30, 1973, Mary, Maureen, and I began our journey to Idaho for a short vacation before starting my civilian career working for Charmin Paper Products in Green Bay, Wisconsin.

Brigadier General James Hamlet presents me with the Army Aviation Association "Broken Wing Award" at Fort Benning, Georgia, June 1973. Mary looks on at right.

XV
CIVILIAN!

The coming transition to civilian life scared the hell out of me. I had no experience at it as an adult. My entry to West Point came one month after my graduation from high school. I'd been in uniform, either at West Point or in the Army, for a total of 11 years, which just happened to be my entire adulthood. Simple things such as how to properly and appropriately dress were daunting to me. I had little confidence that the skills that I'd learned in uniform could be transferred to civilian life. It didn't seem that there was a tremendous need for people to fly helicopter gunships or to command field artillery batteries. I lacked distinguished academic credentials from West Point, and my Army activities hadn't seemed to capitalize on those abilities, meager as they seemed to me. Probably most dispiriting to me at the time was that I didn't have the slightest idea of how to find a job.

Fortunately for me, there were several executive recruitment firms that had found placement of departing military officers to be a good business. One with whom I'd cast my lot had pioneered a concept called the "career weekend." They would invite recruiting managers from 20 to 30 companies to a central location for a weekend. The program would begin with a presentation from each company describing the kind of work they did and what kinds of skills they were looking for. The 200 or so prospects would have provided their *résumés* to the recruiting firm prior to arriving at the event.

At the first such event that I attended, not one single company expressed an interest in my *résumé*. This was not turning out to be a confidence builder. One company, Johns-Mannville, seemed like it might be a possible fit. I signed up to be interviewed by their recruiter. It was brutal. The interview began with rapid-fire questions like, "What do you want to be doing ten years from now?" I responded with something like, "Well, I really don't know; I was really thinking more about a month from now." The interviewer literally browbeat me with questions for which I had no answers. I wanted to leave NOW!

That night I lay awake trying to picture myself working for Johns-Mannville. I'd be going to their asbestos pipe division. What do you do as a manager in a pipe factory? I had no idea. What is it like to have to check the pipe inventory every day? Even as the recruiting managers described the work, I had no frame of reference to which to compare their descriptions. All of my mental sketches were pictures of sheer drudgery. Was there any possibility that I could adjust from the pace and the responsibility level that I'd had in the Army to the drudgery of daily checks of pipe inventory?

As it worked out, Johns-Mannville was the only company with which I interviewed at that first weekend. After my emotional and mental battering at their hands, I couldn't bring myself to schedule another interview with another company...and, frankly, I simply didn't find them very interesting. I needed to regroup.

Several weeks later, the same recruitment firm scheduled another career weekend in another city in the region. I approached this one with the same feeling of trepidation that I had at the previous event.

One important thing was different, however. This time one of the companies, after reviewing my *résumé*, sent me a message that they'd like to talk to me. I signed up for the interview. It was with Charmin Paper Products Company of Green Bay, Wisconsin. From their "Mr. Whipple" television commercials, I knew that they were a toilet paper company. That was a business that I'd certainly never considered, and I had no idea of how the business operated.

The interview was in the room of one Mr. Jim Crawford. Jim was, in comparison to my previous interviewer, very laid back. We talked about many non-business subjects. He seemed like he simply wanted to get to know me. The conversation turned to my adventure of being shot down in a Cobra by an SA-7. Jim was genuinely interested in the story. I told him every detail of what happened and what I'd done. He seemed in awe. By the time I finished this tale, we had run out of time. We talked about nothing else...nothing to do with my skills and abilities, nothing about what kind of work I might be doing...nothing! I felt like I'd blown another interview.

A few days later, I received a phone call by which I was invited to come to Green Bay to spend a day touring the Charmin Paper Mill.

The long and the short of it was that at the end of the day, I was offered a job as Team Manager for a production crew operating two paper machines. It was the first of several doors that the act of being shot down would open for me.

Charmin Paper Products, which was a subsidiary of Procter and Gamble, was a straight shooter company. They didn't promise the moon but where commitments were made, they delivered. I was given three months to develop and complete a program of self training. My progress was evaluated weekly, and I was given regular, honest feedback. At the same time, I was allowed complete freedom in scheduling my training activities. At the end of the training period, I was well positioned to take over my new responsibilities.

I learned early that paper machines were a lot like helicopters. They were machines that consisted of motors, gearboxes, drive shafts, lubrication systems, hydraulic and pneumatic systems, and control systems. The level of detail of my knowledge of the helicopters that I had flown in the Army had served me well, and similar knowledge would serve me well in the paper mill environment.

Similarly, I found that crew leadership in an industrial environment required people skills not so different than those required for managing and leading soldiers. Respect for people's dignity along with basic adherence to the Golden Rule provides a pretty good base for leading in any environment.

At home, Mary and I (mostly I—Mary was more a natural at it than I) were learning how to become neighbors in a suburban, middle-class setting. Most of our neighbors were about our age, so the joining up process was fairly smooth. Maureen quickly found new playmates, and our second daughter, Laura, was born a few months after our arrival.

As well treated as I was by the company, my transition wasn't without its stumbling blocks. In some cases I was able to adjust quickly; in others, I stumbled along not fully understanding all of the dynamics of my environment. Many of these impediments were in the area of socialization.

When I went to work at Charmin, I was almost 30 years old. Most of my peers were between 5 and 8 years younger than I. In many cases, they entered the company immediately after college. Their experience did not include anything remotely similar to the experiences that I'd had in seven years in the Army.

My own age group was generally one level higher than I in the management hierarchy. A few had had military experience, but most had not. Many of them had taken advantage of the various types of draft deferments that were available. Quite a few had made a case that their work at Charmin was critical to U.S. defense interests. Although I never questioned it openly, I found it interesting that manufacturing toilet paper was somehow critical to national defense.

For various reasons, some of which I'll never really know or understand, my Army and Vietnam experiences would not be good conversation starters. In fact, in most situations they would be quite the opposite. As I reflected years later on that social environment, I would state it thus: "If you wanted to empty a room quickly, a good thing would be to start to talk about Vietnam." Such anathema wasn't confined to my work environment. Indeed, it permeated the country. America wanted to purge Vietnam from its memory.

As a result, I began to leave my Army and Vietnam experience to the past—as best I could.

But Vietnam wouldn't go away. In early 1975, North Vietnam, once again, invaded South Vietnam. This time the ARVN would be without American air support or advisers—they would be going it alone. But owing to the Paris Peace Agreement, they could count on American material support. America had promised that.

The South Vietnamese government committed several strategic miscues which led to panic in the north of the country. The television news footage from Danang was disturbing. Scenes of a panicked mass of Vietnamese on the tarmac at the Danang airport were dismaying. The South Vietnamese, hoping to consolidate their forces, ceded the north of the country to the invading North Vietnamese.

I wondered what it must be like to be so precipitously abandoned by one's government. The North Vietnamese continued to push southward, but there were heartening reports of South Vietnamese resistance, most notably at Xuan Loc about 40 miles east of Saigon. Reports from there described an intensity recalling An Loc.

In the U.S. President Ford asked the Democrat-controlled Congress to authorize funding to provide promised material and ammunition to the South Vietnamese. The Congress refused. South Vietnam was doomed. On April 30, 1975, the North Vietnamese entered Saigon.

I was sickened. So much had been sacrificed by so many. We had won the "hearts and minds." The ARVN had demonstrated a capability and a will to fight. The American government betrayed an ally. More importantly, it had betrayed the sacrifices of its own military. I felt it personally.

At work as the months and years passed, I was able to accumulate skills, abilities, experiences, and relationships that would help me to redefine myself as a business professional.

Charmin was a good experience overall. A year or so after I joined, the company became fully integrated into Procter and Gamble. I learned the nuts and bolts of the business, and I felt that I was held in reasonably high regard by those with whom I worked. Having the name Procter & Gamble on my *résumé* was a bonus.

After four years of working at P&G, a recruiter called me at home one evening with a prospect for changing companies. As it happened, the new company, Potlatch Corporation, was in northern Idaho, where Mary and I were from. The chance to return to our roots was attractive. It was made more attractive by the fact that we had just gone through a Green Bay winter notable for the fact that in one 54 day stretch, the highest temperatures recorded were less than zero degrees Farenheit. Lewiston, Idaho was described regionally as the "Banana Belt." It wasn't a no-brainer, but it was close.

XVI
BOAT PEOPLE

Our family was in Lewiston for eight years—from July 1977 until September 1985. While there, we were able to become reconnected with both Mary's and my extended families. Maureen and Laura were both able to begin relationships in the family, most importantly with their many cousins.

One of the important changes was that Mary was able to go to work. A local college, Lewis and Clark State, became a site for a commercial Intensive English Institute. Mary had done some academic and practical work in linguistics while in college, and she was employed by the institute as an instructor in English as a Second Language (ESL). Among her first students was a large group of Venezuelans. Many of them arrived in Lewiston with no knowledge of English. There were few Spanish speakers around; however, I had had Spanish at West Point. I was able to help with some of the logistics of settling in the new students.

About the same time, I was finding my work in the paper business to be less challenging and less fun. As I considered the future in my work environment, I became increasingly frustrated. I felt that one way of making my work more interesting would be to combine it with the interests that my contacts with Mary's students had sparked. Ultimately, I thought that I might be able to make myself valuable to a paper company doing business in Spanish speaking countries. In my free time, I began to immerse myself in Spanish language materials. I enrolled in a college program in Hispanic cultures. That involvement inspired me to talk with my family about vacations in Mexico and Spain, which we took, and we thoroughly enjoyed them. The end result was that Scott Paper Company found me an attractive match for a position at their manufacturing facility in Mexico near Mexico City.

While in Lewiston, my Vietnam experiences became less a factor in my life and that of our family. There was, however, one important exception.

About a year after our arrival in Lewiston, we began to hear reports of increasing numbers of Vietnamese who were desperately fleeing Vietnam. Many of these people were people who had had some past ties to Americans during the war. The North Vietnamese had started what were called "reeducation camps," to which "disloyal" Vietnamese were being sent. At best, these camps were punishment camps. At worst, they were death camps. Fearing for their lives, many thousands of Vietnamese attempted to escape by whatever means possible.

Most of them left the country in whatever watercraft they could find or cobble together. Many of these craft were not seaworthy, and the luckier occupants were rescued at sea by friendly ships. Most of them were temporarily settled in refugee camps in Thailand and Hong Kong and other friendly countries in Southeast Asia. These people became known as "Boat People."

As I began to hear about these people, I felt an urge to assist in some way. I retained strong feelings about how our country had betrayed them, and I thought that maybe by becoming involved in some way with relief programs, I could do something to help to offset what I considered the wrong that we'd done them.

To my surprise, the subject came up one Sunday morning at our church. There had been an inquiry to the church as to whether they would be interested in sponsoring a Boat People family. At this point, we weren't well known in the church, but I didn't hesitate to encourage as forcefully as I possibly could a program to sponsor some Boat People. A congregational meeting was scheduled to discuss the subject.

At the meeting there was much resistance to the idea. Much of the resistance was for very good reasons, much of it quite correctly pointing out the difficulty of cultural adjustments In what was a fairly remote agricultural area. It was a hard sell. But I sold hard. I explained to the congregation some of my own views about how America had committed itself to the Vietnamese only to betray them in the end. I talked about how our country had won the "hearts and minds" battle and how the fleeing Vietnamese were regarded as traitors in their country, even to the point of being shot at as they left.

Either my impassioned pleas worked or the congregation simply wanted to shut me up. They voted to support a family.

The difficulty of the task softened suddenly. Almost instantly, we fashioned a support infrastructure to address the most critical needs. Mary would work with the family on their English skills. A local farm family not affiliated with our church heard of what we were doing and volunteered a set of living quarters. A supermarket manager offered a job stocking shelves in his store. Others would coordinate donations of household materials and clothing.

The family that came to us was from a small town in the countryside. None of them spoke or understood a word of English. None of them had had any exposure to western culture. The head of the family, a man named Huy, had run a small produce business in their village. His pregnant wife and his sister were with him. He was a quick study in the job that was offered to him at the supermarket.

The family adapted quickly to their new surroundings, and our church's project was viewed as a success. After a time, the family learned of relatives who had been settled in a larger Vietnamese community in California. Our church and community were saddened by their departure but pleased by the success of the family and of the efforts of our congregation.

XVII
MEXICO

I arrived in Mexico City for my new job as Engineering Services Manager at Scott Paper Company's local affiliate on September 9, 1985. My work would be in a pulp and paper mill located 22 kilometers north of the center of the city. There were two other Americans working in the plant, and there were usually one or two Scott engineers on site for special projects. Each morning, we would car pool to the plant, leaving from the hotel where I was temporarily staying.

On the morning of September 19, ten days after my arrival, I was on my way to work traveling with three other American employees of Scott Paper Company. We were proceeding northward on *Avenida Insurgentes*, the main north-south route through Mexico City. We were about halfway to work when our car began to shake. It felt as though one or more of the wheels had come loose. After a few seconds, the shaking stopped. About the same time, a transformer on a nearby utility pole exploded. None of us in the car had any idea what had happened. About 20 minutes later, when we reached the plant, several of the people at the entrance to the plant asked us if we'd felt the earthquake. Only then did we know what had happened. We subsequently heard via radio reports that many downtown buildings had collapsed and that many people had died.

We left work early that day. We knew that international communications were completely down and that the international airport had been closed. At that time, Mary and our daughters had not yet joined me in Mexico. I was unable to contact them to let them know what had happened and that I was OK.

As we drove back into the city, we were impressed by the spontaneity of the reaction by the city's youth. They had, at various points around the periphery of the city's core, set up coordinating points where information was being exchanged and volunteers with vehicles were provided with directions about where they might proceed in order to be most helpful. Most of the city's communications and security infrastructure had been destroyed, so the initiative of these mostly adolescent people was very needed and timely.

Notably absent from any of the areas through which we passed was any sign of a government response.

For the next several days, the city and much of the country were shut down, but I was able to walk into the most heavily damaged areas of the city. I was reminded of my experience during the 1968 Tet Offensive in Vietnam.

The smell of decaying human flesh was an odorous blanket over the worst areas. It recalled my experience patrolling near Saigon in 1968 when, as we patrolled from approximately 20 kilometers outside the city toward its outskirts, we were constantly smelling the odor of hastily buried NVA/VC bodies.

As I wandered, I noted the expressions on the faces of the Mexicans that I encountered. Again, it recalled the expressions that I'd seen nearly twenty years earlier on Vietnamese faces as disaster broke upon them. It's difficult to precisely define the expression. It's a sort of mask that people put on. It may be shock. It may be anger. It might be determination. It might just be a blank stare. It's probably all of those things. One thing it probably isn't is fear. I was seeing these people, in Mexico City and previously near Saigon, at a time when they were convinced that the worst of their fears had already been realized. I continued to notice that expression a month later when I walked with Mary through some of the most damaged areas of the city.

The earthquake reminded me much of what I'd come to know of human resilience. Again, in many respects, it was a replay of the same kind of resilience that I'd seen in the South Vietnamese following Tet 1968.

Overall, I was left with a very positive impression of the Mexican people. At their most desperate moment, they seemed to come together as a great national family. That unity extended beyond themselves. I was extremely impressed by several acts of kindness shown to me, a *Gringo,* who happened to be in their midst.

My work during the next four years was extremely satisfying and rewarding. The team of expats of which I was a part was able to contribute much to the improvement of Scott's Mexican operation. Along the way, we were able to contribute much, also, to environmental and economic improvement far beyond the limits of our specific business.

Likewise, our family enjoyed what was probably one of our most satisfying experiences together. We were all fascinated by the cultural amenities offered by the city and the country. Additionally, all of us were able to form friendships with many Mexicans and other expats from other countries.

XVIII
RETURN TO VIETNAM

Our four years in Mexico was followed by a year in the U.S. We purchased a home in south New Jersey from which I commuted to a Scott Paper plant in one of Philadelphia's third-world suburbs. Maureen had graduated from high school in Mexico City and had gone on to Pacific Lutheran University in Tacoma, Washington. Mary, Laura, and I gave it our best to adapt to South Jersey. We all suffered from culture shock. When one leaves the U.S. to live in another culture, one is prepared to make accommodations to new and strange things. When we return, it is natural to expect to find things as we left them. Unfortunately, the country doesn't remain static while we're gone. The longer we're gone, the more things change. During our four years out, much had changed. A couple of months after settling in to our Jersey home, the three of us realized that we missed being overseas. We all wanted to do it again! I informed the powers-that-be at Scott that, should an opportunity to return to expat life turn up, I'd definitely be interested.

Several months passed, Mary found a job she liked, and Laura made some close friends at her high school in Woodstown. Just about when they were pretty well adjusted and satisfied in our new environment, I was notified of a plant manager opportunity in Bangkok, Thailand. The transfer meant that they'd have to give up some valued relationships with people and work, but, in the end, they were ready for the new adventure in Southeast Asia.

I relocated to Bangkok in September 1990, and Mary and Laura joined me there immediately after Christmas that year.

Mary and Laura both integrated quickly into their respective expat communities. Mary became volunteer editor of the National Museum Newsletter, and Laura quickly made friends with kids from all over the world at International School Bangkok. For me, Thailand was mostly about work. The positive was that as Plant Manager, I was expected to be a regular participant in regional activities. The company had offices in Hong Kong, Taipei, Tokyo, Seoul, Singapore, Kuala Lumpur. I was able to travel to most of those locations plus mainland China.

One destination that was not on the company's agenda was Vietnam.

When the 1991 Christmas holiday season was approaching, we discussed what we'd like to do during the Christmas season. We seemed to reach a consensus that several days of jet- lag going and several days of jet-lag returning probably weren't worth the few days that we'd actually spend with family in the States. It seemed that we were all in favor of an opportunity to have a leisurely look at how Asians spend Christmas (Thai department stores start putting out Christmas materials in October). The matter had seemed to be put to rest when Laura asked one night, "If we're going to stay in Asia for Christmas, why don't we go to Vietnam?" I think that my jaw may have hit the floor with an audible thud.

After a couple of days of thinking about it, I finally thought, "Well, why not? We'll probably never have another chance, and, besides, the idea of having an 18-year old daughter that's actually interested in something like this is a good thing."

At the time, U.S. law prohibited travel of U.S. citizens in Vietnam. We would not be able to make the trip using our normal documentation. Some friends in Bangkok told me about a British-run travel agency that had been able to book travel for some Americans in the past. This wasn't your normal travel agency in the lobby of the downtown Hilton. It was a pair of scruffy Brits who had a room over a bar in a Bangkok flesh-pot area called Soi Cowboy. Soi Cowboy was a short three-block walk from our apartment on Sukhumvit Soi 19, so I wandered over one afternoon after work.

Basically, it was all pretty simple. The Brits would put together some phony documents for us to use instead of our U.S. Passports (Use of our passports would result in them being stamped by the Vietnamese government, thus providing evidence to U.S. authorities of our illegal travel). We would book a package through them that would include our airline tickets, our hotels in Vietnam, and a van with driver and "guide."

I was able also to arrange our itinerary through the travel agents. We would fly to Tan Son Nhut via Royal Thai Airlines. We would spend a couple of days in Saigon.

After that we'd go to Vung Tau, a former U.S. Rest and Recuperation center on the coast about 50 miles south of Saigon. After that, we'd head north again, passing Long Thanh and Bien Hoa, and heading north on National Highway 13. Highway 13 would take us through Lai Khe, Chon Thanh, and Tan Khai to An Loc. Of course, all of those places had great meaning to me.

The flight to Saigon was fairly short, so our maximum flight altitude was fairly low—probably no more than 15,000 feet. The weather was clear, so I was able to observe the geography as we went. Cambodia was still under the Khmer Rouge and it was considered a hostile place by the Thais, so our flight followed the Cambodian coastline until the border with Vietnam. Upon reaching the Vietnam coast, we flew inland to the northeast across the Mekong Delta toward Saigon. My combat travels had never taken me to the Mekong Delta, so I found it an interesting place. At the time, the ground looked very dry and brown. It did not appear that much agriculture was going on. It was not what I expected.

As we began our approach to Tan Son Nhut, the area began to appear much more urban. We touched down at Tan Son Nhut on Runway 07—southwest to northeast. As we rolled down the runway, I couldn't help the feeling that nothing had changed since I was last there in 1972, almost twenty years before. As we turned off the runway, I looked at the cracks in the concrete, and I remarked to Mary, "The same thistles are growing out of the same cracks as twenty years ago!" The bigger surprise was when I could see the tarmac in front of the old military hangars. Parked in front of the hangars were C-130s, C-123s, Hueys, A-37s, and A1Es. It looked exactly as I remembered it; it looked like nothing had been touched. It began to seem downright spooky!

The plane taxied to the terminal—the same terminal that I'd been in and out of in 1972. It was hardly bigger than a bus terminal in an eastern Montana cow town. This was the terminal of the major airport in the country!

Inside the terminal we went through the line for immigration. Everyone made their best attempt at regarding us as if seeing Americans was a normal part of their routine. We were treated very courteously. Next we went to baggage claim. Baggage was sent into the terminal on a conveyor that passed through an X-ray machine. The machine was attended by five Vietnamese men. It broke down on every other bag that passed through it. The result was that it took about an hour and a half to process all of the luggage.

About half way through our wait, I suddenly heard, seemingly singing at the top of her lungs, Karen Carpenter, doing "We've Only Just Begun!" I was startled and turned around to see, about 7-8 feet up a vertical steel column, a Pioneer speaker. It was one of those huge speakers that had been available in the PX during my last combat tour. There was some evidence of a larceny concern as the speaker was clamped tightly with a steel strap that was welded to the column. I looked about to try to locate a second speaker, but there was none (maybe there had been one, the loss of which occasioned the heavy steel strap on the remaining one). Clearly we were not getting the Carpenters in stereo.

After finally receiving our luggage, we were ready to leave the airport. After some brief confusion, our guide and driver showed up. They had a white Toyota HiAce van similar to one that was assigned to my plant back in Bangkok. We loaded the luggage into the van, and left Tan Son Nhut. Everything looked very familiar as we left. I'd taken the same route through the same neighborhoods a couple of times during my second tour in 1971-1972.

Our primary guide was a young twenty-something who spoke reasonably good English. We learned that his father had been an ARVN Captain during the war. Our guide also had no hesitancy about letting us know that he was a member of the Communist Party— something that he communicated with noticeable pride. He was clearly very pleased and enthusiastic to have the job of showing us around. He had a habit of affirming everything that I would say with, "Yeah, right," or "Quite right." Although it was unsaid, it was also clear that he had a dual role—he would be our tour guide, and he would be our "minder."

We arrived at our hotel—one that I hadn't heard of; it was called the hotel Que Huoung. It appeared to be one of the few fairly newly-constructed buildings that we saw. Our room was on the third floor—on a corner that overlooked a street corner. It was high enough to afford us a very good view of the streets below. There was a balcony on one side. It was clear that the room, actually a small suite, was probably one of the nicest that the hotel had to offer.

We spent quite a long time standing on the balcony observing the street scenes below. The streets were quite busy with pedestrian and bicycle traffic. There were a few motorcycles, a few trucks, and almost no cars. There were also Lambrettas. These vehicles which I'd commonly seen in the countryside during both of my tours were like gas-powered golf carts. They were three wheeled, and the driver rode a single seat in the front where he steered with handle-bars. The back of the vehicle was a flat bed that sometimes had bench seats and a roof over the seats. As they had been during my two tours, these vehicles, used for transportation of people and goods, were the basic commercial vehicles in Vietnam.

As a family, we'd spent quite a lot of time in foreign countries, but we were, nonetheless awed by the exotica which we observed below. Huge baskets of flowers were being transported on bicycles. Several times we'd see people moving 2-3 one-hundred pound bags of rice on their bicycles. It recalled the stories that I'd heard of the NVA transporting rice down the Ho Chi Minh Trail by bicycle. Here was living proof that it could be done.

We were also at an elevation that we could clearly see the electrical wires that supplied the various establishments along the street. The utility poles were made of concrete, and the insulators were positioned wherever they could fit. Wiring generally showed many splices, and it was clear that it would not meet the codes of most countries. Some of the wiring looked suspiciously like Army issue commo (communication) wire. After an hour or so, we met with our guide to discuss our itinerary. The first thing that he told me was that we would not be able to visit An Loc. When I inquired as to why, he responded that the government remained concerned about something that he called the "hot, hot summer" that had occurred during the war. "Hot, hot summer?" I asked, "What was that?" He answered that it was a very big battle that occurred in the 1972. He said it had caused much suffering. "I know," I said, "I was involved in the battle, and being able to go there is, to me, one of the most important parts of this trip."

Truong, our guide, told me that he would see what could do to allow the visit. I wasn't optimistic.

We spent our first full two days on guided tours of various sights around Saigon—the Ho Chi Minh Museum, the former National Palace, a walk by the former U.S. Embassy, a water puppet show which railed eloquently about the historical misdeeds of the Chinese, and other items which, though interesting, might not have topped the lists of most tourists.

Between tours, we were allowed to walk about without escort. We found Saigon to be very threatening. Beggars were very aggressive. Most were children, but they operated in swarms. We'd be walking and suddenly we'd be surrounded by 10-15 children, all asking for money. On one occasion when we were surrounded by such a swarm, one young boy managed to unzip the pouch that I was wearing on the front of my belt. Fortunately, I saw him just in time.

On several occasions we hired "cyclos" for sight-seeing. Cyclos are a uniquely Vietnamese form of rickshaw. Usually, they have two passenger seats, side-by-side, in front of what appears to be the back half of a bicycle. Some of the passenger seats are quite elegant. We soon learned that many, if not most, of the cyclo operators were ex-ARVN soldiers. Many had suffered at the hands of the North Vietnamese and had spent time in the reeducation camps. Most spoke enough English to be able to let us know that they desperately wanted to share their stories. Several gave us addresses to their homes and invited us to visit. Given the controls around our visit, we chose not to do so. It was, particularly to me, very moving to witness this desire to share their experiences.

Our next stop in our itinerary was Vung Tau. Vung Tau is a resort city on the coast about 50 miles south of Saigon. During the Vietnam War, it was an in-country rest and recuperation center for the U.S. military. None of the hotels were particularly luxurious in their heyday, but Communist rule had apparently regarded them as bourgeois excesses, and they were all in varying states of deterioration. Ours was no exception. The bathtub in the bathroom was clearly an after-thought. It was a tub set into what was formerly a shower stall. The tub drain didn't line up with the shower drain, so a piece of pipe was affixed under the tub drain in order to divert drain water to the shower drain a couple of feet away. Aesthetics didn't count for much as long as it worked.

The highlight of our Vung Tau visit was midnight Mass on Christmas Eve. There was a large Catholic Church in the city, and our guide graciously arranged to fulfill our request to attend midnight Mass.

About a half hour before Mass, our guide met us at our hotel. We were transported to a street facing the side of the church, away from the main entrance. We were then escorted to a small door leading to the sacristy of the church. There, we met the priest who would be conducting the Mass. He spoke good English, and we carried on a reasonable conversation, but he was clearly nervous about our presence. Just before the Mass was to start, our guide escorted us out of the sacristy, across the altar, and into the sanctuary. The church was huge. At the right front of the sanctuary were three empty pews. A small sign in Vietnamese said, "Reserved for Foreigners." By this time, it all seemed pretty bizarre. Three empty pews in an otherwise packed church would contain Mary, Laura, me, our guide, and our driver.

Things would get more bizarre. The parishioners thought we were Russians. There had been some indications of a major oil find in the South China Sea, and a large number of Russian petroleum engineers had been sent to Vietnam in order to assist in developing the find. They all lived in Vung Tau. It didn't take us long to learn that it was much better that we were American than Russian. The Vietnamese despised the Russians. One fairly inebriated Vietnamese man made his way to our pew where he spent several minutes haranguing Laura, apparently about the evils of being Russian, before he was provided some assistance in departing.

The Mass was beautiful. A Vietnamese choir sang a number of carols and hymns. Most were quite beautiful. After the Mass we were escorted out in the same manner in which we entered. Clearly, we were to be kept totally separate from any contact with the Vietnamese attending the Mass.

It was a totally bizarre experience.

Next on our agenda would be An Loc. Truoung, our guide, had informed us that the authorities had relented and would permit a visit to An Loc, after all. I was pleased. An Loc would be a day's drive from Vung Tau. We'd travel the Vung Tau—Saigon highway northward to Bien Hoa where we'd cross the Dong Ngai River toward Phu Loi and Phu Cuoung, both cities with which I was familiar from my first Vietnam tour with the 1st Infantry Division. At Phu Cuoung, we'd join Highway 13 for the trip north to An Loc.

Most of the area around Bien Hoa, including the formerly sprawling U.S. Army base at Long Binh, bore little resemblance to anything that I remembered. Long Binh showed no indication that it had once been the largest U.S. military installation in the country. It had the same randomness about it as did the countryside which surrounded it. It was difficult to find exactly where it had been.

Bien Hoa was familiar only because of a small knob of terrain that stood at the west end of the runway of the massive airport that the U.S. had built there. Of course, we were not permitted to see the former Bien Hoa Air Base.

From Bien Hoa, we crossed the former Binh Duoung Province, passed Phu Loi—which I found totally unrecognizable—and stopped for a great lunch at a restaurant perched over the bank of the Saigon River at Phu Cuoung.

At Phu Cuoung we picked up a second guide. He was Luoung Van Vo. Luoung had been a Captain in the South Vietnamese Army. He had spent several years in "re-education camp." Apparently, the re-education hadn't taken very well. Luoung was, by profession, a mathematician. The government had wanted him to teach mathematics in schools; however, Luoung refused to do so, feeling that by practicing his profession, he would be providing assistance to the Communists. He had made a small living, however, tutoring mathematics students on an individual basis. As the government began to liberalize, it began to see advantages in attracting western tourism, including Americans. Luoung, an English speaker who had been trained at Fort Bragg, was invited to become a tour guide for the newly- demarcated Song Be Province. [22] He accepted the job, as he told me, because he felt that it would provide an opportunity to work to change the country from within.

After lunch we began the trip up Highway 13. We'd pass through Ben Cat, Lai Khe, and Chon Thanh before arriving at An Loc. Much of the area along the highway had been improved since the war. There were many more permanent buildings made of cinder block with metal roofs replacing the open buildings with thatched roofs with which I was familiar.

Highway traffic was a mish-mash of everything that one could imagine in Southeast Asia: many bicycles, lots of small motorcycles, lots of Lambrettas, some water buffalo drawn carts, and a very few cars. There was no lane discipline, and the smaller vehicles simply darted in and out wherever they pleased. Our driver drove through all this at about 30 miles/hour, beeping his horn 3-4 times a minute.

As we proceeded north from Lai Khe, we encountered the first of three large convoys of logging trucks. The trucks were converted from U.S. Army 5-Ton and 10-Ton trucks. All of the convoys were huge. In one of them, I counted more than 70 trucks. Each of them carried loads of very large logs. On some trucks, the logs were of such great diameter that only three of them could be carried. Our guides explained that the trucks were hauling the logs to the port in Saigon. They would be loaded onto ships for shipment to Japan. They further explained that the export of logs was one of the few ways that Vietnam had to attract foreign currency to the country.

As we continued northward, the impact of the logging became quite apparent. In both of my combat tours, I'd become very familiar with the countryside on either side of Highway 13. During my first tour, I'd spent much of my time patrolling the jungles with U.S. Infantry. I had

---

[22]Song Be Province was a new Province after the Communists reorganized the country. It included portions of the former Binh Duoung, Binh Long, and Phuoc Long Provinces. Some of the key cities in the new province were Lai Khe, Phuoc Vinh, An Loc, and Song Be (Phuoc Binh).

memories of jungles with double and triple canopy so thick that daylight at ground level was scarce at mid-day. All of that was gone. In some areas, the jungle had been so thoroughly stripped that one had an uninterrupted view of 4-5 miles on either side of the highway. In many areas, the jungle had been stripped and replaced by rubber plantations. That the jungle had been so thoroughly stripped was a shock to me.

Lai Khe looked vaguely familiar as we passed through on Highway 13. Again, had I not known that a major military installation had existed there 20 years previously, nothing there would have caused me to suspect it . Chon Thanh was the next major town, and it was one of the few places that I saw in the country that actually looked better than I'd remembered it. I had remembered it as a quite rustic place with mud and thatch buildings with a lot of charcoal fired kilns. Now, the buildings were clearly permanent, and there were some fairly attractive and well-kept yards and grounds. The town was also much larger than I'd remembered it.

North of Chon Thanh was Tan Khai. The Tan Khai of my memory was nothing more than a hamlet. I'd been there on Med-Cap operations in 1967. I'd fired rockets into it from my Cobra in 1972. It was from near Tan Khai that the SA-7 that had brought Marco and me down during the battle for An Loc was fired. We stopped. I f we were among the first Americans to visit Vietnam in 20 years, no one in Tan Khai seemed to notice. We bought a couple of Cokes at a local market. People there were reasonably cordial, but cool. Certainly no one betrayed any indication of recognition!

It was a short distance from Tan Khai through a rubber plantation to An Loc. Our visit was another bizarre data point in a lengthening series. I had hoped to be able to see what had transpired in a city that I had remembered as a scene of total destruction. That hope would not be fulfilled. As we approached the city, our guides seemed visibly nervous.

Having walked around An Loc and its surroundings quite extensively during my first combat tour, and having flown over it fairly extensively during my second tour, I was very familiar with our surroundings as we approached the city. At the south end of the city, Highway 13 crosses an east-west road at the north edge of a rubber plantation. Just past the intersection is a Catholic Church. When we approached the intersection, the driver turned the van crossways in the highway. We could look north along the highway as it entered the city and served as the city's main street. At some distance, I was able to see the two story brick schoolhouse which had served as a significant landmark during the An Loc battle. It had been one of the few buildings that was left standing after several months of shelling. Our guides dutifully pointed to the statue of Christ that stood in front of the Catholic church by the intersection. It was still severely pock-marked by shell fragments. The head was missing —blown off by U.S. bombing we were told. I knew better. Virtually all of the damage done in An Loc had been done by North Vietnamese artillery which featured nightly barrages of up to 10,000 rounds during the battle. I didn't figure this was the time to argue about it .

During the time that we were there—no more than five minutes—we were not allowed to get out of the van. We could view the main street of the city only from the van. Nonetheless, it was pretty obvious from the structures that we could see that the city was far from recovered from the battle of twenty years earlier.

I do not know exactly why our guides were so obviously nervous. Over the years, I'd heard of a guerrilla effort by former Saigon military members after 1975. Given the horror visited upon An Loc by the North Vietnamese during the 1972 battle, it was not too difficult to speculate that the city had not yet been fully pacified by the Communists.

After our brief glance at An Loc, we were spirited off to the east toward Quan Loi. Again, there was little evidence remaining of a military installation. Our guides referred to it as "Tecnica." We sped quickly by the place, with our van kicking up a healthy cloud of the area's red laterite dust. Occasionally, we'd see small groups of Montagnard women pedestrians along the road appearing much the same as they had when I encountered them on infantry patrols nearly 25 years earlier.

Some distance past Quan Loi we reached our destination for the evening. We were told that it was formerly a French resort. I recalled having seen sets of buildings marked on our 1:50,000 scale military maps that were labeled as resorts, but I'd never actually seen them. In this case, the location was near a lake called Soc Xiam. There was an old pier leading out to a gazebo-like structure in the lake. The lake was not particularly appealing as it was choked with water hyacinth and other flora. One would suspect that there were probably some interesting fauna in the lake as well.

Near the lake, we reached a group of chalet-style buildings in a clearing next to a fast flowing, high volume stream shrouded by jungle trees and plants. It was a beautiful and idyllic scene. We had arrived around mid-afternoon, so there was going to be some time to do some exploring.

It was quickly apparent that we were the only guests at the resort. The only other people there were members of a family that ran the place. They lived in one of the buildings on the site. There were three or four chalet type lodges of various sizes. The largest of them would be our lodging for the night.

We were checked in by a teen-age girl who spoke no English, but our guides were able to translate for us. It went quickly, and we were shown to our chalet, which from the outside appeared to be reasonably nice. When we went inside, it became more interesting. The first thing that struck me was that in the main bedroom, there was a hole at the top of the wall where it butted to the ceiling just above the head of the bed. From the hole down the wall, it appeared that there was a bit of a trail made by small feet. I guessed that it might be a rat trail. I said little. There was a small refrigerator and a window style air conditioner, which was running, mounted in one wall. The floor was apparently a bare concrete slab. I say apparently because it was difficult to tell; it had a hardened glaze that was made of an accumulation of filth that appeared to be nearly an inch thick. This is no exaggeration! A second bedroom, presumably for Laura, seemed to be a sort of an after-thought. It had a light bulb hanging from the ceiling, but it was difficult to judge its cleanliness because it was so dark. We didn't immediately explore the bathroom except to learn that the toilet was one of those older types that was equipped with a water closet some distance up the wall above the toilet. It was flushed by pulling a chain connected to a valve on the tank.

After a short while, the manager came to greet us. He spoke some English. We learned that the electricity would be shut off between midnight and 6:00 a.m. That meant that we would have neither lights nor air conditioning during those hours. The manager told us about the attractions at the resort. There was a trail that one could walk in order to see the entire site. One feature was a small zoo which featured a barking deer. There were several other smaller native animals. Also featured was an old "guerrilla" base camp. The manager spoke of guerrillas almost disparagingly. The base camp turned out to be an old bomb crater with a poorly constructed bunker on one side of it.

The conversation with the manager revealed that he had not been there long. He'd previously been a foreman at one of the nearby rubber plantations. He'd had some kind of a run-in with the local authorities which resulted in his transfer to become the resort manager. He lived at the resort with his family, and it was clear that he was not pleased with his current lot.

We decided to walk the trail and see the sights. The manager's teenage daughter was apparently our "minder." As we walked she lurked about 50 feet behind us saying nothing. Occasionally we'd try to engage her, but she'd simply avert her gaze in another direction. Still, whenever we moved, she moved. I'm sure that she was probably concerned about our safety!

After touring the grounds, it was supper time, and we had a great meal featuring some kind of roast beef and vegetables. It was truly delicious.

As in all tropical areas, darkness came quickly, and by the time we were finished with our supper, it was dark, and the mosquitoes were out. We returned to our room. We had some matches and candles to see us through the night after the electricity would be turned off.

Of course, there was no radio or TV. Fortunately, we all had sufficient reading material to pass some time. I decided that it would be good to check out the bathroom facilities with a view toward a possible shower. Forget that. There was a shower, but there was no drain, and the piping apparently wasn't connected to a water header, for nothing came out of the faucets.

There was one lightbulb hanging by a wire from the ceiling above the wash basin. There was a faucet on the wash basin, but it hadn't apparently been used in some time as a large spider —larger than the diameter of the drain—had taken up residence over the drain. His estimate of the drain's utility was pretty accurate, because there was no drain pipe connected to the bottom of the wash basin.

Aside from the bathroom's obvious lack of minimal facilities, it was fithy and smelly. None of us would opt for even a sponge bath that night. Given the state of the second bedroom we began the evening on the bed in the main bedroom with all of us choosing to remain fully clothed. When the lights went out at midnight we sort of began to sleep. Somewhere, around 3:00 a.m., I sensed something running along my body and down my leg. Then it seemed like it ran back up my leg. It didn't take a lot of imagination to conclude that this was at least one rat. He seemed to find my leg an interesting area for he made several trips up and down it. This continued sporadically for the remainder of the night.

Obviously, none of us slept that night.

The next morning we had an excellent breakfast after which we got in our van for the trip back down Highway 13 to our hotel in Saigon. Since it was our second view of the countryside, there were few surprises....a few more convoys of logs and the driver's cassette tape which seemed to have *Take My Breath Away* copied as every other song. It's one of those things that takes a long time to get out of your head. I'm still working on it more than 20 years later!

After an overnight in Saigon in which we dined sumptuously on steak and french fries at Maxim's in the old Majestic Hotel, we wound our way through the city back to Tan Son Nhut and our Royal Thai Airline flight back to Bangkok. The outbound "wheels up" off the runway was nearly as relieving an experience as it was 25 years previously. For myself, I thought, "Whatever curiosity I might have harbored about Vietnam has reached my lifetime satisfaction." I feel confident that Mary and Laura felt the same.

XIX
SOUTHEAST ASIA TO SOUTH AMERICA

A few months after our Vietnam journey, I learned that Scott Paper Company was beginning the first of several "downsizings" that it would undergo before being acquired by its rival, Kimberley-Clark. The precise meaning to me was that my position was essentially being eliminated. More disconcerting than that was that there was no new position in the States to which I would be transferred. My transfer was to outplacement. Such was the life in the paper manufacturing business in the 1990s. It was, for sure, a disorienting, disconcerting experience.

Our return to the U.S. presented us with some other transitions. Laura had graduated from high school, and she had been accepted at Cornell University. Maureen had graduated from Pacific Lutheran University, and she was about to marry Sean, a friend whom she had met while in school. Being "between" jobs definitely had its puts and takes.

In the fall of 1992, I learned from a friend about a plant manager opportunity in Venezuela. After some mutual "feeling out" with the search firm over the telephone, Mary and I went to Venezuela to check out the job. We never go anyplace without causing a ruckus. The week prior to our visit, an obscure Lieutenant Colonel in the Venezuelan Army had led a *coup d'etat*. His name was Hugo Chavez, and by the time we arrived, *El Comandante* Hugo was safely ensconced in some prison.

We spent just over two years in Venezuela. My assignment was a truly unusual plant manager assignment. The plant was a large facility located, quite literally, in the jungle. The facility included a company town with a population of about 4,500. There was a school, a church, a club/restaurant, a store, a bank, athletic facilities, and, of course, a pulp and paper mill. The Venezuelan-owned company was part of a group that was owned by one of Venezuela's "thirteen families." There was much that was fun and interesting about the assignment.

What wasn't fun was my gradual discovery that I had encountered a web of corruption that rivaled anything that I'd ever seen. It was systemic in a way that I hadn't previously seen, and it involved many people in the plant, the corporate office, the government, the military, politicians, and businesses. About the only people it didn't involve were the workers in the plant.

As my awareness of the pervasiveness of this cancer developed, I resolved that, rather than "going along to get along," my best course would be to be seen as incorruptible. My presence there represented many institutions and people. Complicity would represent a betrayal, not only to my own values, but to those of many others. For starters, I was aware that, though my position had no official standing, I was a *de facto* representative of the United States. I was also a West Point graduate, cloaked with all the meaning that that represents. Above all, I believed that there was a body of workers under my control and supervision whose expectations of me did not include my becoming part of the existing scenery.

Over time, I found myself in positions in which directions given to me increasingly carried with them the requirement that I become a participant in activities that I found to be beyond my ethical boundaries. In such cases, I opted to either ignore the direction or to manipulate it in such a way that my ethics would not be compromised. Obviously, this led to complications in my relationships with upper management and beyond. Ultimately, it became a concern for personal safety, both for me and for Mary. At that point, I made the decision to leave the assignment and to return to the United States. Coincidentally, a newly-elected Venezuelan government made the decision to release one Hugo Chavez from prison. Interesting times were becoming more interesting.

XX
REPATRIATION AND RECONNECTING

On March 1, 1995, Mary and I were "wheels up" at Maiquetía Airport near Caracas. Our sense of relief was nearly equal to that which we experienced when departing Saigon's Tan Son Nhut Airport a little more than three years earlier.

We returned to our home in Alloway, New Jersey where I would, once again, bury myself in a job search.

Ultimately, I would be employed by Brown and Root Forest Products Company, a division of Brown and Root, which was a subsidiary of Halliburton Corporation. I don't recall my exact hire date, but it would be easy to find as my first day coincided with the commencement of Dick Cheney's tenure as the company's Chief Executive Officer. Cheney's appointment somehow garnered a lot more press coverage than did mine.

Implicit in the job was the requirement to move to Houston where Mary and I made our home for the next seven years.

Shortly after settling in in Houston, I began to expand my knowledge of personal computers. Although I had a very high comfort level with these machines, I had been overseas almost continuously for ten years. There had been many advancements in software and communications while I was out. My work at Brown and Root would require me to improve my knowledge rapidly. My natural affinity for these machines had spawned a hobby-like interest in them, so I didn't mind.

One of the areas of cyberspace which I sought to explore was a relatively new structure called the Worldwide Web. I had set up my PC in our home, and it was connected to the internet almost immediately after our arrival.

Sometime in mid-1996, during an evening of web surfing, I stumbled into a website called Yahoo! It was quite intriguing. The hierarchical structure of the site proved to be logical and easy for me to navigate.

From the home page, I found a link for "Government." When I clicked on that, a link for "Defense Department" appeared. After that, it was "Department of the Army, " and so on. I drilled down through "Army" and "units" until I arrived at a link for "Blue Max."

I clicked on the link, and, Voila! Immediately, the picture shown below with its caption filled my monitor:

The Survival of Captains Mike Brown and Marco Cordon

Copyrighted art by Joe Kline

I was dumbfounded. For a moment, I sat mesmerized and unbelieving. I had neither seen nor heard of the picture until that moment. I studied it for another minute. It was so real that I wondered if it weren't a photograph. I was amazed by its accuracy and detail. It was a perfect representation of what had happened to Marco and me on June 21, 1972. The copyright notice affirmed it as Joe Kline's painting.

Mary was in another room. I'm sure that my eyes were heavily glazed as I went out to tell her, "Come here; you have to see this!" She was equally amazed as I explained to her, "That's exactly what it looked like!" Like many others, Mary had had trouble visualizing what had happened based on my inadequate verbal descriptions.

As I continued to scroll below the caption, I saw a transcription of the audio tape that I had recorded on the morning after the shoot-down 24 years earlier. I read the transcription, and found it to be 100% accurate.

As Mary and I continued to gaze at the monitor, we wondered who was responsible for the picture and transcription being on the Internet. Ultimately, I determined that it was an organization called "Blue Max Aerial Rocket Artillery Association." There were no names on the page with which I was familiar; however, there were several e-mail addresses which I noted. I wrote messages to several of them, introducing myself and suggesting further contact.

When I returned home after work the following day, Mary told me that I'd had several telephone calls. One of them was from a person named Mike Sloniker. When I returned his call, his immediate reaction was, "Where the hell have you been?" I didn't know Mike Sloniker, and I didn't know if he was referring to the past hour or to the past twenty years.

I didn't know Mike Sloniker from Adam. After briefly telling me about his own background, which included serving as Operations Officer of A Company, 229th Assault Helicopter Company during the Battle of An Loc, he told me of his enduring interest in the shoot-down of Marco and me. It had seemed that the the story was drifting slowly toward oblivion with the passage of time. The Army had used my tape for several years as a training vehicle, but newer helicopters, newer threats, and newer enemies had allowed our story to be on course to become a historical footnote.

That changed in 1993 when an Apache unit bearing the nickname "Blue Max" was activated at Fort Bragg, North Carolina. The resurrection of the unit nickname Blue Max was an occasion for a reunion of F Battery, 79th Artillery. In preparation for the reunion, Mike contacted an aviation artist friend by the name of Joe Kline and asked him to do a painting which would depict our shoot-down. Mike furnished Joe with the names of several ex-Blue Max pilots who had been eyewitnesses to the event. Through a process of witness interviews and trial and error, Joe was able to produce his incredible painting.

Joe's painting attracted a lot of attention. An ex-Blue Max crew chief by the name of Russ Warriner had started a website for an organization that he had started called the Blue Max Aerial Rocket Artillery Association. He used the painting for the home page on the website. It was his website that I had stumbled onto when I was drilling down through Yahoo the night of my discovery. I also found that the painting figured prominently on another website belonging to the Vietnam Helicopter Flight Crewmembers Association. None of the principals of any of these sites or organizations had any idea where I was or what had become of me.

Among the first questions that I asked Mike Sloniker during that initial conversation with him was, "Do you know where Marco Cordon is?" Mike responded almost with disbelief, "Well, yes, he's down in Texas right near where you are!" I asked for Marco's contact information, and Mike agreed to find it and send it to me by e-mail the next day.

After receiving Marco's contact information, it occurred to me that I really didn't know much about him. I had retained a mental picture of him that included a diminishing hair line, a face that wore a smile as default, and a fairly slightly built fellow. It was conceivable that, except for mission related exchanges pertaining to our June 21 experience, we might never have engaged in another conversation. I had, for 24 years, hoped to be able to talk with him about our experience; but now, as the reality of our conversation finally approached, I had no idea what to expect.

Actually, I wasn't completely in the dark. I knew that Marco had participated in the 1993 reunion at Fort Bragg. He had been an enthusiastic participant in the group that provided the input for Joe Kline's painting. I knew that Marco felt that our experience was important, and he wanted to assure that it was granted its proper place in Army Aviation history.

So, after 24 years I nervously dialed the phone number in Round Rock, Texas. I was consciously trying to throttle my desire to pour out my thoughts and emotions that had accumulated over the years. Both of us knew that a phone conversation couldn't possibly convey the thoughts that we wanted to share. Only by meeting face to face could we hope to possibly close the loops that were so abruptly left open as we separated on the Lai Khe airstrip so many years before. Marco's son, Marco, Jr. was a senior attending Texas A&M University. An Aggie homecoming football game was scheduled for October 19, 1996, at Kyle Field in College Station. We agreed that meeting there with our wives would probably work best for all of us. We planned to meet several hours before the game in order to get reacquainted and in order for our wives to get to know one another as well. I don't recall whether central Texas was in the midst of one of its typically legendary droughts that year, but if it was, our meeting was probably a salubrious event for the Aggie campus. Indeed, the tears of the four of us probably watered most of the territory that we covered that day.

The events of the day were a blur. We were seated high over the northeast corner of the football field at Kyle Stadium. Kansas State won the game, but, not being a partisan for either team, I wasn't too focused on the game. Most of the game was spent thinking of questions that I'd stored up over the years and asking them of Marco.

We did manage to learn much about one another. I learned that Marco was of Guatemalan parentage and that he was bilingual in Spanish. Given my cultural immersion of several years in Latin cultures, we clearly shared some common interests beyond our experience in helicopters. We found that we were immediate and fast friends. At the end of the day, we knew that the day was the beginning of a long friendship between the Cordons and the Browns.

The following year, several Blue Max veterans decided to hold a reunion at Louisville, Kentucky. Marco and I both made plans to attend. We agreed that we would make our flight reservations on the same flight from Houston to Louisville. Flying together would give us the chance to become even better acquainted and to strengthen the bond that we'd established at College Station. There was also a symbolism that was manifest in the two of us arriving at the reunion together.

1997 Blue Max Reunion in Louisville (l-r): Bruce Hendricksen, Ernest (Fast Eddie) Rickenbacker, Jay Perry, Marco Cordon, (unk), Bill Baskett, Art Jetter, Nick Molea, Al Russo, BG Dave Funk, Bill Leach, Warren Chunn, Jim (Jet) Jackson, Larry McKay, unk, BG Tom Garrett, Mike Brown

he reunion was a sort of bittersweet closure for many of us. We celebrated our continued, genuine comradeship along with our well-documented record of extraordinary achievement and collective valor in combat. At the same time, we shared our continuing sense of loss and sadness for our nine comrades who perished during the An Loc battle.

The reunion was also a manifestation of something else. That was the fact that by the mid- 1990s, the internet had become available to virtually everyone. My own reconnection was really only an example of something that was going on much more broadly. E-mail distribution lists focused on a variety of interest groups were springing up in virtually every sector of society. These were structured in such a way that anyone who became a member of a group could communicate instantly with each and every other member of the group.

Among Vietnam helicopter pilots, at least two such groups were formed. One was called the Vietnam Helicopter Flight Crewmens' Network. The other was called Heli-vets. Many helicopter vets belonged to both groups. The groups provided a forum in which members could share memories, compare memories, validate memories, and discuss a variety of other topics. The groups provided many of their members with a communications outlet that many had never previously had.

Previously, social barriers had taught many veterans to remain reticent and withdrawn with respect to describing their Vietnam experiences. To some the need to to measure their sharing in broader forums was frustrating. The new, online forums provided an outlet in which Vietnam Veterans, including aviators and crews, could express themselves with a candor and openness not previously experienced. It was, for many, a liberating experience in which we were confident that our thoughts were being shared with people who, because of their shared experience, would appreciate and understand what we were expressing or trying to express.

In some ways, this new connectivity was a two-edged sword. While it generated a new comfort level for many of us, it also had a seductive quality. The balance between risk and reward that governed our exchanges clealy shifted from the former to the latter. For many, there was an addictive quality to these new cyber communities. The volume of messages exchanged assured that huge amounts of time would be consumed, and the psychological reward of belonging to the communities invited participants to greater and greater participation. The time that pilot veterans spent in cyber conversations was the subject of more than a few cordial dialogs between spouses.

The intimacy of these conversations was probably most dramatically exemplified by one of our comrades who continued to exchange e-mail while lying on his death bed in the UK. He was writing messages to his comrades until his final hours. Ultimately, his death was announced to the group in an e-mail which his partner composed a few minutes after he expired.

For me, participation in these on line forums was immensely satisfying and rewarding. There was a continuing curiosity about my shoot-down, and the positive recognition that I continued to receive kept the forums enticing.

I had actually met a very few of the participants, but it seemed that I'd gained a great number of new friends. The openness that characterized these forums gave participants the feeling, if not the illusion, that we knew each other very well.

Once in a while, while I was living in Houston, online friends would pass through town. My friend, Mike Sloniker, would often steer people visiting Houston to me, and we'd meet somewhere for a beverage or a meal.

Often it seemed like Mike was acting as my agent. In addition to steering traveling comrades to me, he'd often put me in contact with people who had reason to be researching subjects including helicopters in Vietnam, the Battle of An Loc, or information about specific individuals.

One such occasion was in May of 1998. The family of Michael J. Blassie, an A-37 pilot was pressing the Department of Defense to confirm the identity of the soldier then buried in the Tomb of the Unknown Soldier. The identity was confused by the fact that evidence that was found with the body suggested that it could have been either 1LT Blassie or CPT Rodney Strobridge. The *Washington Post* was preparing a feature on the situation, and part of the article was going to be a profile of each of the men. While I hadn't witnessed the shoot-down of Rod Strobridge and Bob Williams, I felt like I knew Rod well enough to describe him for the feature. It was important to me that he be portrayed in the way that I remembered.

The *Post* did the article which appeared as a Sunday feature. It treated Rod's memory very favorably and cited specific comments that I had made.

Ultimately, DNA tests confirmed that the body was not that of Rod, but that of LT Blassie. Rod, who had been promoted to Major, continued to be carried as "missing in action." In the intervening years, his status has been changed to "Killed in action—body not recovered."

Another occasion on which Mike Sloniker directed media attention to me was in 2002. He had been contacted by Fox News which was planning a program called, "Helicopters in Vietnam" on the Oliver North series, War Stories. Mike was in contact with the producer of the show and had told him that no program about helicopter operations in Vietnam could be complete unless it included my story. Mike must have been an effective salesman because the producer contacted me, expressing great interest.

At the time, I was living in Houston. Fox News provided me with transportation and lodging in order for me to meet at their studios in Washington, D.C. with Oliver North. I was not without mixed feelings as I approached the Oliver North interview. I'd watched several of the War Stories programs, and I felt that they were well done. Many of them showcased the deeds of military veterans who had not otherwise been recognized. At the same time, the memory of LTC North's controversies with Congress over the Iran- Contra affair continued to lurk in my mind.

Whatever doubts I might have had, my reconciliation was that by doing the interview, I would be representing many others who deserved the recognition that the interview would bring. It would bring new notice to Blue Max and its members and their deeds. I also recognized that there were very real conflicts of great consequence with which LTC North was forced to deal. These conflicts would have tested the mettle of anyone, and I was glad that I had not been presented with questions of such enormity or complexity in my own experience. While my thoughts on this issue were serious, I wasted little time in resolving them.

My meeting with LTC North was a pleasure. He was a good interviewer, and he knew the right questions to ask. As two combat veterans, there was little need to test one another's understanding of expressions and terminology. He was also quite knowledgeable about helicopters, including Cobras. The interview lasted a little more than half an hour, and I was very satisfied with it.

After the interview, North asked me about my schedule for my return flight to Houston. He offered his car and driver for transporting me to Reagan National Airport. Before leaving me with the car and his driver, we would drive to a radio station where he had a regular afternoon talk radio show. The drive lasted about twenty minutes, and it allowed me an opportunity to know LTC North better.

In getting to know each other personally, the fact that we were both service academy graduates was a natural ice-breaker. Although he was a year older than I, North had entered the U.S. Naval Academy a year after I entered West Point. He began with the Class of 1967, while I was in West Point's Class of 1966. Due to an auto accident, North was forced to sit out a year at Annapolis, and he ultimately graduated with the Class of 1968.

Almost immediately after beginning our conversation, he asked me if I'd known Henry Spengler of West Point's Class of 1967. I responded that, indeed, I had known Hank, but not at West Point. I then told him that I'd flown with Hank in the Blue Max in Vietnam. I also told him that I was probably the closest eyewitness to Hank's crash at Loc Ninh after he and Charlie Windeler had been shot down.

North told me that he and Spengler had developed a close friendship after they had been buddies during respective "exchange" weeks between the two academies. They'd continued their friendship, and had corresponded and met fairly frequently on social occasions for several years following their initial meetings. As he recounted what he'd heard about Hank's shoot-down, it became clear to me that he'd received quite a bit of erroneous information. I described in detail what I'd seen at Loc Ninh on April 5, 1972.

We continued the drive with general conversation about current events, mostly about international affairs and the military. We agreed on most subjects, and I felt quite privileged to be able to pick the brain of someone who was so clearly well-informed.

North has made it his passion to see that our military's heroes are duly recognized. He told me several times that it's his greatest privilege to be able to talk with America's heroes on a daily basis. His work with Fox News, both as the host of War Stories and as a combat correspondent, has assured appropriate recognition to countless men and women who might not have been so recognized. I respect that, and we Veterans are in his debt. He has, indeed, landed on his feet.

Fox News broadcast "Choppers in Vietnam" on June 16, 2002. All friends and family were duly notified, and many presented their uniformly positive reviews following the broadcast. It was an honor in its own right for me to appear on the program, but the caliber of the other people who were on the program with me heightened that honor. The billing included General Hal Moore and Colonel Bruce Crandall who were featured characters in the then recent movie, *We Were Soldiers.* Mike Sloniker and several other helicopter veterans also appeared.

Before the broadcast, Fox had notified a local newspaper, *The Olympian*, of the broadcast. They'd also provided them with a tape of the broadcast. We had moved only a few weeks before to the Pacific Northwest from Houston, and, except for a few family members, we knew no one. *The Olympian* sent a reporter to interview me about my experience and about the program. The resulting article was a feature in the Sunday, June 9, 2002, edition.

The *Olympian* article provided me with wide exposure in the local area. Former comrades in the local area saw the article and called me on the telephone. Several organizations called me and asked me to do speaking engagements, which I did. Within a few days, I found myself with many local friends and acquaintances, something that ordinarily would have taken years to develop. The recognition that the publicity had provided me opened many new doors for me as we settled into our new environment.

XXI
CONCLUDING THOUGHTS AND MEANING

As I said at the outset of this story, my overriding goal has been to share an experience and how it has affected my life. If someone finds some historical value in what I have written, then that's great, but it's not my purpose. The story of my shoot-down has captured enduring interest that surprises me, but to me the most valued part of the story is its aftermath and how it has shaped and continues to shape my life. About that, I'd like the reader to indulge me a few thoughts.

First and foremost, the events of this story are part of a broader spiritual journey. I suspect that, in that respect, my experience is not totally unique. Life's journey for most of us follows some fairly well-defined patterns.

When I was shot down, I had reached my 28th year only one week earlier. At that age, I was pretty convinced of my ability to control my destiny. As you've read, there were plenty of reasons why I might have questioned that conviction. The business of aerial combat against an enemy who is also pretty convinced of his righteousness is one in which situational control is tenuous and frequently at risk. I've tried to share here my awareness of that and its effect on me.

Nonetheless, after I was shot down, I was, perhaps, taken in by the amazement that others expressed about what I'd done and how I'd done it. I'd prepared a factual, recorded statement of what we'd done, and it captured the attention of others. A question that frequently arose during discussions of the event went something like, "Did you feel or sense the hand of a greater power in influencing your successful outcome?" From my vantage point forty years later, I'm astounded by what I remember of my responses to that question.

My response usually went something like, "No. I had a plan that I'd thought through for such a contingency, and I followed the plan." I'd state it with all the conviction that a cocky 28- year old could muster.

Thinking back to those words after several decades' reflection, my immediate reaction is "How arrogant!"

The growth that continued learning and experience have provided me has certainly shaped a different view. If anything, I'm much more in awe of the event than I was then. My awe is not for what we did—we simply did what we could with what we could control. My real awe stems from my greater appreciation that there were so many variables over which we had absolutely no control which went right. Any of those variables, had they not been favorable, could have resulted in disaster. They could have caused disaster even if Marco and I had managed all the controllables perfectly. One example that came to my attention recently is that Marco, while discussing the event with someone else, said that he considered jettisoning the rocket pods, but he decided against it because he thought the loss of the pods would shift the center of gravity forward to an extent that maintaining the fuselage at a level attitude would not be possible. After hearing this, I looked at the position of the pods as compared with the probable location of the center of gravity, and I concluded that his fears were justified. This is important because I actually did attempt to jettison the pods, but because there was no electrical current, my attempt failed. The uncontrollable factor was the unavailability of electricity. It prevented me from doing something that, had I done it, could have been disastrous.

There were many other "uncontrollables." The critical point that I wish to make here is that in order for Marco and me to survive, we had to do the controllables right; but the uncontrollables had to go right also....and they did.

There are very few experiences in life—I'm taxed to think of any in my own life—in which all of the elements over which one has no control go right. In this case they did. The sheer improbability of that occurring convinces me that some power beyond Marco and me was at work.

Having made the conclusion that some power greater than us determined the outcome of our situation, the obvious question then becomes, "Why?"

If I had the answer to that question, I would not be writing this story. I'd be writing a much greater one. I was given a second chance, and I do not know why. What I do know is that my story is part of a larger personal journey, and that larger journey has led me to an ever increasing faith. My faith is larger, more certain than it was when I was 28 years old—or 48 years old or 58 years old. If there is a purpose to my several second chances, I'm not likely to recognize it by pursuing it. I believe that purpose lies somewhere in the growth of my Christian faith. I've been blessed with more second chances than I deserve, and my worthiness will ultimately be measured in my faith. I have a long way to go.

Another lesson that I frequently share is one about the will to live. A few years ago, my friend Mike Sloniker shared with me the idea that in an emergency—particularly in a life-threatening emergency—if a pilot has something that he can move, he has control of something. It was another way of stating the same lesson that I learned in my after dinner discussion with Harry Davis a couple of weeks before my shoot-down: "You fly the airplane until you can't."

I'm told that the Army distributed copies of my audio tape to aviation units for training purposes for several years after my crash. No one has shared with me their exact training purpose, but I suspect that it has something to do with providing trainees with an example of how someone survived a crash previously considered unsurvivable by following the dictum, "Fly the airplane until you can't." I've never hesitated to use my experience as an illustration of the validity of that thought.

I also believe that that principle extends to many other areas of life. I have, on occasion, visited hospital patients whose disease or injury has brought them face to face with the reality of their own mortality. That realization can, if allowed to, have a very depressing effect on the patient's outlook, even to the point of reducing their prospect for recovery. In such situations, I try to find and share those variables that the patient "can move" in order to possibly gain a sense of control over their situation.

One of my most rewarding and inspiring recent experiences has been to watch my daughter Maureen's battle with breast cancer. After her initial diagnosis was reclassified to Stage IV, she didn't panic or wallow in self-pity. Rather, she seemed to calmly take inventory of all the things over which she could possibly gain control. She seemed

135

almost to organize a team about her in order to gain control of her situation. Part of that organization was to determine all the information that she would need. Another part was to communicate her needs to her family, her friends, and her co-workers. She integrated her medical team into the broader scheme. I don't know if this was simply a natural reaction or a structured effort or both, but it was obvious, and it seemed to work. Her approach, along with the prayers of literally hundreds, contributed to her confronting her disease and its demons in an exemplary and positive way. She had, perhaps for the first time in her life, been confronted by her mortality. She wasn't ready to surrender to that, and proceeded to take control. It works.

Another area that deserves a few words is the subject of courage. Everyone who has been in combat has had to deal with that subject. Our culture teaches us to venerate courageous behavior. Our traditions teach us that it is expected of the soldier in combat. What courage really means is often ill-defined. Many of our conceptions of courage project an idea of fearlessness. That idea has been carried to America's battlefields at varying levels throughout our history. One of the difficulties that a soldier new to war encounters is that no one really trains him or her on what courage "looks like." The concept is left to culture and tradition. Consequently, many soldiers arrive at the fight with a concept of courage that is based on the unreal behaviors that they may have learned in books or in the movies. We learn that fear is something to be beat down, and that to show fear tempts shame.

Both of my Vietnam tours were spent in roles that most would regard as "the point of the spear." My first tour was spent mostly in the field, frequently on patrols looking for the enemy. When we encountered enemy—or when he encountered us—the frequent result was an exchange of fire. The intensity of these exchanges varied according to the mission, the number of troops involved, the weather, and many other factors. Put simply, I was "shot at." My second tour as an attack helicopter pilot was no different. The nature of the mission of an attack helicopter pilot requires him or her to fly into areas where getting shot at is inherent in the mission.

It is a tense life, and for most sane people, it involves fear.

I don't believe that one gets used to fear. It's not an area in which practice improves one's ability to overcome. Most of the time fear is rational; we fear something because a real threat exists. The level of fear depends mostly on the magnitude of the threat and the ability one has to control that threat. During the An Loc battle, the magnitude of the threat was at a level not previously experienced by Army helicopter pilots. The magnitude was measured in the presence of nine battalions of enemy anti-aircraft artillery at the battle. It was further defined in the sophistication of the weapons and control systems in the hands of the enemy; they were state of the art for the Warsaw Pact at the time. The introduction of the SA-7 missile simply intensified an already intimidating threat. Counter-measures for Army helicopter pilots lagged the enemy's sudden increases in capability.

I've written of the feelings that I often had while waiting at Lai Khe for missions to begin. The butterflies and doubts were personal, and I tried to keep them that way. There was little discussion with others. One wouldn't want to betray fear and invite scorn. Years later in discussions with others, I learned that others went through the same struggles. Such struggles inevitably cause us to question our courage. Too often, I think, such questions result in self-doubt. If not reconciled, the doubt can fester into a torment—particularly if such doubts are associated with circumstances in which a comrade or friend gets killed. I wrote earlier of my second-guessing about my performance when Charlie Windler and Hank Spengler were killed.

For me, all of those doubts were erased with my shoot-down. My courage was not an issue with others, and it wasn't with me. If confronting odds that are stacked against you and winning represents a victory over fear, then the shoot-down served to reconcile any doubts— at least for my part. In that respect, I consider myself lucky. Too many of our soldiers leave the battle burdened with these doubts. There is no reconciling mechanism for most. They are left to their own resilience in order to weather the torments that they carry from the battlefield. Too many have failed.

Military medicine has, in recent years, vastly increased and improved its understanding of the psychology of battle and its aftermath. In spite of the often shrill, too politicized criticism of military medicine, I believe that military medical community is doing a superb job of developing its knowledge and managing the psychological wounds of war.

I could not conclude this story without a thought about my continuing connections with my wartime comrades. As I've alluded, our comrades at arms have seen us at our very best, and they have seen us at our very worst. It is the nature of combat that the peaks are lofty, and the valleys are deep. Combat exacerbates the magnitude of both. When you know that your comrades have been spectators at your worst, and they choose to remember and remind you of your best, there is no greater fellowship. Outside of marriage, there is no other human institution where our souls are so openly on display to others. There is truth to the saying that those who have not known combat will never know the bonds of those who have depended so intensely upon one another. It is the reason that when I hear of a reunion of my Blue Max comrades, barring insurmountable barriers, I will be there. In all of my associations in every aspect of the life that I've been so privileged to lead, my comrades in Blue Max remain the finest group of individuals to which I have ever had the privilege of belonging.

XXII
WHERE ARE THEY NOW?

Marco Cordon, after hospitalization at Brook Army Medical Center for treatment of his back injuries, spent approximately one year on convalescent leave. Ultimately, he returned to Army Aviation and flew Hueys in the El Salvador civil war in the 1980s. Following his military service, he continued flying helicopters for a civilian company called Air Logistics which provides aviation support to oil industry operations in the Gulf of Mexico. About five years ago, I asked Marco when he would retire. He responded, "When I can't pass the physical!" Marco loves flying. He and his lovely wife, Marybeth, live in Round Rock, Texas. Marco has retired, and he spends much of his time attending to family affairs in Texas and Guatemala. He is an active member of a BMW car club. The Brown family and the Cordon family have become fast friends, and there is frequent contact between the two families.

Larry McKay passed away on August 6, 2013. After returning to the United States following Vietnam, he continued his Army career, retiring as a Lieutenant Colonel in 1978. His assignments included command of the 101st Aviation Battalion at Fort Campbell, Kentucky and a tour as a professor in the Social Sciences Department at West Point. After retiring from the Army, Larry served as a visiting Professor of Economics at The Citadel. He also served as a board member for several corporations. In 2006, Larry was honored as Alumnus of the Year by the School of Business Administration at the Citadel.

Ron Tusi was tragically killed in a Cobra crash in 1974. At the time, Ron was testing the first generation of aviator night vision goggles. Few individuals have so single-handedly done more to advance their profession than Ron. His widely known and respected successes in destroying tanks during the Battle of An Loc probably rank as one of the most significant individual efforts contributing to the continuing development of the attack helicopter as an effective weapon against enemy armor. His contributions have been permanently recognized and memorialized with his induction into the Army Aviation Hall of Fame in 1983.

James F. Hamlet returned to the United States to be promoted to Major General. He subsequently commanded the 4th Infantry Division at Fort Carson, Colorado. In 1983, he, like Ron Tusi, was inducted into the Army Aviation Hall of Fame. He passed away from cancer in 2001. Throughout his life, he continued to be a friend to all who had served under him during the Spring Offensive of 1972. I was truly honored to have him present my Broken Wing Award in 1973.

There is an ongoing effort to locate the Huey crew from B Company, 229th Assault Helicopter Battalion that rescued Marco and me from our crash site in the jungle near Tan Khai. In the summer of 2012, I received a surprise telephone call from *Bill Wright*. Bill was the Aircraft Commander on the Huey. Much of what I have written about our rescue either originated from conversations with Bill or was verified by him. Bill lives in Indianapolis, Indiana.

Connecting with Bill led to locating the Huey Crew Chief, *David Vaughn*. Dave lives near Midland, Michigan, and he works for DOW Chemical Company.

Neither Bill nor Dave is able to recall the name of the co-pilot or the door gunner of the crew that rescued us.

We'll keep trying.

APPENDIX I

Transcription of audio tape which I made on June 22, the day after Marco and I were shot down:

(This transcription was provided by Mike Sloniker. It is an exact replication of the audio tape with no further editing)

On 21 June 1972 I was working on a mission in support of an ARVN airborne brigade in the vicinity of the village of Tan Khai on highway 13 approximately 6 miles south of An Loc. We were escorting a US slick unit that was tasked with extracting the ARVN airborne brigade from Tan Khai for redeployment.

In support of this, we had a heavy fire team, 3 AH-1G's Cobras. I was the AC of chalk 3. The method of support was to put one ship low with the lift flight and two ships high to provide overall area coverage. Chalk 2 and 3 in the heavy team were the high birds. I was chalk 3. On my second gun run into the area, in which I was providing suppressive fires, I broke to the right and made a pass from SE to NW breaking right over Highway 13 and was in the process of rejoining chalk 2 and taking his wing position, when I was struck by a SA 7 missile.

So far as I know, no one else has survived in a helicopter, anyway, this type of anti-aircraft fire. I think there was a combination of things that accounts for the fact that I am alive and my pilot are alive. And I don't want to underestimate the importance of luck which was the most significant contributor to our good fortune was luck. I do feel, however, there are some things that we did, that we had not done, the luck we had would not have been able to save us. In describing the impact of the SA-7, but first let me back track a little bit, I think the single most important thing that happened was the fact that other personnel in the area, other aircraft in the area, were able to observe the missile being fired. As they observed it, they yelled, "missile, missile, missile!" over the VHF radio. I think the fact that I knew what I was hit by, and what the aircraft should do was the single most important contributing factor, outside of luck, in my survival.

141

I feel every unit, or every task force, that is operating in an area where SA 7's are known to be, should have an SOP on alerting aircraft when a missile is fired. They should also have posted in such position as to advise or observe 360 degrees around the flight as possible, so that these can be seen.

After hearing the words, "missile, missile!, I looked over my left shoulder, I saw the signature of the missile, I thought it was heading for my aircraft. Just as I saw the missile, I saw it hit the aircraft. Probably at the same time as it was hitting my aircraft, I was rolling off my throttle, and bottoming my collective pitch.

The impact of the missile on my aircraft did not seem to be that severe. There was concussion, but there was not as much as one might expect. I would say judging on the way it felt to me, as far as concussion was concerned, there was probably not more HE charge in the warhead of the SA 7 than there was in a 40MM grenade.

What happened to the aircraft as it hit, is the tailboom was totally severed, completely severed in the vicinity of the battery compartment, which on the Cobra is directly below the exhaust stack. The aircraft, as soon as it was hit, jostled slightly, it seemed to pitch up and pitch down and from side to side. This was followed by, during the autorotation, the aircraft began to spin about its mast to the right at a nose low attitude. As the aircraft descended, it spiraled, making a spiraling descent, continuing to spin slowly about the mast. The speed of the spin was, I would say, about the same angular velocity as one would experience in a normal rate pedal turn.

I did not look at any of my instruments after being hit. Shortly after I was hit, as soon as I was hit, I lost all radio communication. I had no radio communication what so ever. I did, however, have intercom with my front seat. Using the intercom, I instructed my pilot, CPT Cordon, to empty the his turret weapons system, fire it out. He attempted to do so, but was unable to do it. My control movements, during the descent, were very few. Having been aware, for some time, that this could happen, I had thought, pretty well thought it through, what I would do, if I were hit by a SA-7, and my tailboom were severed. It seems to be characteristic of the missile that it does severe the tailboom, if it strikes you from the side. I felt the biggest

142

problem that I would have with no tailboom would be the CG shift. That it would be most difficult to prevent the nose from becoming extremely low. particularly in a loaded helicopter. And this would have to be the biggest problem I would have to cope with. As it worked out, that was exactly the case. I told my self, that if this were case, and prior to the crash, I told my self, that my action would be to pull complete aft cyclic and attempt to correct for the CG shift. This I did; it did not prevent a nose low attitude. Those who observed my descent said I appeared to be descending a skids level attitude; however, I felt that I was nose low. I attempted to experiment with the cyclic enroute to the ground. I tried slight left and right cyclic movements which did little for me, and as far as I am concerned, were a waste of time.

I feel that anybody that has the same misfortune, that I had in flight, should attempt to only pull aft cyclic. Their only concern should be CG. As far as cyclic movement should be, I bottomed the pitch and I left it that way. I made no attempt to control RPM. I made no attempt whatsoever to select a forced landing area. There was no way I could have controlled the aircraft to bring it to a forced landing area. Probably if I had selected a forced landing area, I probably would have not made ot anyway, even if I could have guided the aircraft to it. I'll explain the reasons for this later on.

During the descent, RPM built; as it built, I felt feedback forces in the cyclic and the collective. The cyclic tried to pull itself forward, I pulled it back and I was able to keep it against the rear stop during the entire descent. The collective attempted to push it self up, I was able to keep it on the bottom, until my pitch pull.

Also during the descent, a couple things I tried to do, were trying to fire out my turret, I was able to see that I was not able to adjust my CG. I attempted to jettison my wing stores, my wing store jettison did not function. I suspected, as I thought about this prior to my accident that it would not, since the wing store jettison circuit breakers and your electrical power is largely located in the forward portion of the tailboom.

So my wing store jettison capability was lost, having determined this, I attempted to fire out the remainder of my ordnance. I was 50%

expended at the time. My ordnance, my 2.75 inch rockets, could not be fired. With these three unsuccessful attempts, the turret, the wing store jettison, the rocket firing, all these failing, I abandoned all further hope of slowing my rate of descent, by getting rid of extra weight or by shifting my CG by getting rid of extra weight in the wrong places.

As I said before, the only control movement that I made, cyclic-wise, was to pull complete aft cyclic and held it there and bottomed my collective pitch and held it there.

At about 30 feet above the trees, was where I pulled my pitch. I pulled pitch at about the same rate that I would in a normal autoration, except I pulled every bit of pitch that I had. The collective was full up as I reached the ground. This significantly slowed my descent also assisted in my CG problems. I wouldn't say that I recovered from the nose low attitude, but it recovered somewhat. It also began a violent spin. At this point, I can't remember if the spin went to the right or the left. I do know it was violent, I do know that it was stopped by my landing in the trees.

The second most significant thing that saved me, was the fact that I did land in trees. I had no choice over whether I was going to land in trees or land in an open area. It was something that fate alone could determine. As I said, there was no directional control, there was no selecting a forced landing area. But luck was with me and I did land in trees, which helped me in two ways. One, they stopped the spin of the aircraft, two they assisted in cushioning my fall.

On impact there was no fire, the engine had continued to run. I had rolled of the throttle to the flight idle position initially; however, I did not attempt to make further attempts to shut the engine down. If I had it to do over again, I would probably do that. I would probably attempt to shut the engine down, if I would have had time to do so.

My concerns were, fire and my ordnance exploding; however, my impact was soft enough that the fuel cell, I do not believe the fuel cells were broken, and therefore the fire was not a factor, as it had been in other cases where people come down as a result of a SA 7 strike.

As far as what I did on the ground, I was on the ground for

approximately 10 or 15 minutes. And I don't believe what I did on the ground is of that much assistance to anyone else. Suffice it to say, that I did land in a bunker complex; my front seat and I both made attempts to conceal ourselves until friendly aircraft got in the area, my survival radio would not operate, so we moved into a clear area and waved until we were spotted by friendly aircraft. At this point we concealed ourselves again to await pickup. Other significant things I think that contributed to the success here were, number one, I had only had 600 pounds of fuel on board the aircraft at the time of the crash, and I was 50% expended. I had fired all of my outboard pod, and I believe, a few of my inboard rounds.

As far as feelings, I think the psychology is as important as anything else, as how you survive this thing. There was no question, having been around SA 7 environment, for the last two months, there was no question in my mind, that I was dead on the way down. However, I never gave up. I had enough control over the aircraft to do something for myself. I still had a good rotor, I still had two controls, my aft cyclic and my pitch control, and in the end, the things I was able to do, assisted in saving my life.

I think, probably, the most critical point, is when you come to the altitude where you should pull pitch, the 30 feet or so, you know in your mind, or I knew, in my mind, that I had it, that I was dead at this point on or be dead in a very short span of time. However, I did what I thought I should do anyway, and fortunately for me, it worked out to the best. I hope that by putting these things on a tape and putting them in a place where other people operating in the same environment can have access to what I say, I hope that it will save other lives. I feel, however, that all the elements must be working in one's favor, because they were with me. I feel that, as I said initially in the tape, luck was the biggest factor in saving my life. The aircraft did go to a place, i.e. the trees, where ground conditions assisted in bringing the descent to a favorable conclusion.

There is no question in my mind, that I had I gone to an open area, that the outcome would have been much different. As I said, also, whether I would have wanted to or not, I would have had no control over the aircraft. I will not say it's impossible to survive this type of crash by landing in an open area, I feel now that an important thing is as long as you continue to fly the aircraft, no matter what your situation is, that you use every available control that you have. Every control you have is an asset, you have some chance. I do feel , however, in my case, that the violence of spin after pitch pull, and probably that fairly high rate of descent, I don't believe we would have made out of the aircraft if it had not been for the trees.

Other things that were beyond my control, were the situation factors were the fact that I was 50% expended and that I only had 600 pounds of fuel. Had I had 100% ordnance on board, and a 1200 pound load of fuel, the situation would have been far different.

So again I conclude and say that it is my hope that this tape will do some good, and the right combination of luck and knowing what to do with the aircraft, in the event that this happens to anyone else, that it will result in saving somebody's life.

Thank you.

APPENDIX II

Statement by CPT Marco Cordon, Co-pilot/Gunner

22 June 1972

On the 21st of June 1972 near the city of An Loc, Republic of Vietnam, the AH-1G Cobra helicopter of F Battery, 79th AFA, Task Force Garry Owen was shot down by a surface to air missile of the Strela type (SA-7).

A heavy section of 3 Cobras was flying cover for the lift ships UH-1H's of Co 229 Assault Helicopter Battalion, Task Force Garry Owen. Our mission was to extract a brigade of approximately 1000 men of the 1st ARVN Airborne Division which had defended An Loc for over 60 days.

The PZ for the extraction was located on (Highway) QL 13, near the village of Tan Khai. Enemy forces had succeeded in shooting down two AH-1G Cobras the previous day, one from F/79 AFA, and the other from F Troop, 9th Cavalry, with the loss of four pilots. One of the Cobras was shot down by a STRELA missile and the other by suspected heavy anti- aircraft fire.

Early on the morning of the 21st, the attempt to extract the Airborne troopers was resumed. The first attempt resulted in the downing of a VNAF helicopter with the loss of one crewman. This setback temporarily suspended the operation until 1315 hours, when Task Force Garry Owen UH-1H's supported by Cobras of Blue Max began to extract the troopers. Four lifts of 5 ships were successfully vectored into the PZ while being vectored and given fire support by Blue Max.

At the completion of the 4th lift, the first heavy section of Cobras was relieved on station by the second section. Three extractions were successfully conducted while receiving minimal and ineffective 51 cal fire and small arms fire.

At approximately 1515, while we were covering the flight as high bird from 4000ft, a Strela missile was fired by the enemy and the missile was spotted in flight by one of two Blue Max pilots who sent the warning over the radio, "Missile, missile, missile." In accordance with unit SOP, CPT Brown, the aircraft commander attempted to initiate a sharp left descending turn o break the lock of the infrared guidance system but the missile impacted immediately, almost a split second after we heard the warning over the radio. Upon impact of the missile and subsequent explosion the helicopter momentarily assumed a 30-degree nose down attitude but slowly recovered to a level attitude by aft cyclic application. The helicopter then began to spiral to the right and descend at approximately 1500 FPM. No caution lights illuminated in the gunner's instrument panel. Torque pressure indication was near zero, N1 was 98-99%, EGT approximately 530-580° C and rotor and engine RPM remained well within the operating range of 6600.

It was apparent that the helicopter was in some semblance of control and that with some luck we could land in a fairly open space. As we completed the first 180° of our first turn, I saw the tail boom and tail rotor fly away. As the helicopter descended in its level spiral the aircraft commander asked me to fire the 40mm grenade launcher in an attempt to shift the CG rearward, (our minigun had been inoperative all day) but the attempt was unsuccessful. Next, I thought of jettisoning the rocket pods but decided that this would only cause CG problems and probably nose the helicopter over. So it seemed prudent to let well enough alone. My next thought was to transmit a May Day call on VHF but as spoke into the microphone I received no indication that I was transmitting.

By this time we were fairly close to the ground and I decided to remove my chest armor plating from underneath my safety harness which I did successfully. I next attempted to tighten my seat belt to take up the slack from the removal of the armor plating but only could tighten the shoulder harness.

Upon contact with the trees the aircraft commander began to pull collective to slow our descent, which was effective. The contact with the trees stopped the rotating to the right, sheared the rotor blades, and shattered the plexiglass in the front cockpit. As soon as all movement stopped I opened my hatch and exited the aircraft and went to the right side to open the aircraft commander's hatch. He was trying to shatter the plexiglass on his left and managed to do so just as I opened his hatch.

We both then moved to a small clearing about 5 meters in diameter in an attempt to get away from a possible fire. The aircraft did not burst out in flames although the engine continued to operate at what appeared normal RPM.

Almost immediately the other aircraft from our section located our position. CPT Brown put his survival radio into operation and I dug out my survival mirror to use as a signaling aid. We stood in the clearing and waved our arms over our heads to two Cobras orbiting overhead area, were located almost immediately and soon a UH-1H approached the clearing where the wreckage was located.

As soon as we exited the aircraft we both removed our helmets because it was impossible to hear each other talk or listen for any approaching enemy. The other Cobras from our section fired many rockets, and 40mm grenades about 100 meters all around our position to discourage the enemy. The small clearing contained several bunkers with overhead cover and the ground was littered with C-ration cans.

The UH-H began his approach to the clearing which was obviously too small for it, but the Aircraft commander continued to descend chopping his way through.

APPENDIX III

(Statement by CW2 Ronald L. Tusi in support of ' Broken Wing Award for CPT Michael J. Brown)
(A True Copy except as noted)

5 Feb 1973

To Whom It May Concern:
On 21 June 1972 at 1430 hours, I, Chief Warrant Officer Ronald L. Tusi, (SSN deleted) witnessed a feat of pilot skill that I consider unprecedented in U.S. Army Aviation history. On that day the fire team which I was leading was tasked with repeated missions of extracting South Vietnamese Rangers from battle at An Loc, Republic of Vietnam. In the course of our mission one of my wingships piloted by Captain Michael J. Brown was struck by a Strella (SA- 7) missle [sic]. The missle [sic] severed the entire tailboom and a portion of the battery access and electrical compartment. The AH-1G Cobra Gunship began a spin earthward from approximately 4000'. In such instances it is known that the center of gravity shifts considerably and control is next to impossible. I watched the gunship spiral downward in what appeared to be a controlled descent. Although I did not consider the possibility of survivors, I flew to the crash site. To our amazement, my gunner and I found Captain Brown and his gunner Captain Marco A. Cardon [sic] scrambling from their gunship. I landed in an opening in the jungle some 75 yards away and with my gunner, Captain Harry L. Davis proceeded to the site to offer assistance.

Although I personally spent no more than 15 minutes in all, including route to-at-and return from the downed cobra [sic], I saw that Captain Brown's gunship had sustained no damage with the exception of the canopy which they had to break to make a hasty exit to escape the enemy which had the entire area surrounded. Normal exit could not be accomplished because tree branches prevented opening the canopy.

I feel now as I felt then that Captain Michael J. Brown warrants a Broken Wing Award for his display of superb airmanship. I have written a statement in support of an earlier recommendation for this award but have recently been made aware that it had not been processed and had become misplaced during our unit, F Battery, 79 th Aerial Field Artillery, 1st Cavalry Division standown [sic].

I consider it a grave injustice to Captain Brown and U.S. Army Aviation if this feat is not recognized by the Broken Wing Award.

Although the criteria for the award hints that an aircraft should be returned to U.S. Army inventory, I feel that the uniqueness of the enemy situation and the magnitude of his accomplishment justify waiver of that aspect of the criteria. The are in my estimation reasons for waiver:

> (1) the cobra gunship was completely severed in half, but was in controlled flight through 4000'.
>
> (2) it sustained no further damage on impact.
>
> (3) Captain Brown's ability saved his gunner and himself in a situation that most likely could not have been handled by one-in-a thousand avaitors [sic].
>
> (4) the gunship could have been salvaged had not intense enemy hostilities prevented it.

The above is a sworn and true statement.

/s/ Ronald L. Tusi
Ronald L. Tusi
CW2
USAR
Fort Ord, California 93941

APPENDIX IV

(STARS & STRIPES article by SP4 Jim Smith based on interview at Lai Khe Officers's Club about two hours after rescue)

Red Missile Bags Cobra

Fliers Knocked Down—But Not Out

By SPEC. 4 JIM SMITH
S&S Staff Correspondent

LAI KHE, Vietnam — "Somebody yelled 'missile!' over the radio," Capt. Mike Brown said. "I looked over my shoulder and saw the smoke trail. Then I felt the jolt. It happened so fast I couldn't do anything. The tail boom was blown off and I started spiraling down and to the right. I figured it was all over."

Brown's AH1 Cobra gunship had just broken out of a rocket run at a Communist position about six miles south of An Loc Wednesday afternoon when it was hit in the exhaust stack by a heat-seeking, SA7 "Strella" missile.

The 28-year-old Army aviator from Sand Point, Idaho, was the aircraft commander, and part of a team of "Blue Max" gunships covering the extraction of some 1,000 South Vietnamese airborne troops from a hot landing zone near the town of Tan Khai along Highway 13.

He and his front-seater, Capt. Mark Cordon, who was medevaced to the 3rd Field Hospital in Saigon with possible back injuries, became the first fliers to survive a crash after being hit

CAPT. MIKE BROWN

by the Russian-made, tube-launched missile. The aircraft luckily impacted in some trees and Brown was uninjured.

"I thought my number was up," Brown said over a beer. "I thought it was my turn to get it. I was flying up there every day and just asking for it. I said to myself on the way down that if I

ever get out of this I'd tell other people what I did."

Brown said after he was hit he began "autorotating" the bird immediately. As he spun to the right, nose down at a 45 degree angle, he shut off all the systems and allowed the air to spin the main rotor blade to break the fall.

He tried to jettison his rocket pods to lighten the load. But when the tail section was blown off, the electrical circuits were out. Then he tried to fire his minigun and to expend the rest of his lethal 10 and 17-pound rockets. No dice.

It took 30 seconds for the Cobra to hit the trees, Brown said, "although it seemed a hell of a lot longer than that. Neither of us panicked, though. I'd thought a lot about what to do in this situation and I did it."

About 30 feet above the jungle, Brown raised the nose of the aircraft up so it would impact parallel to the ground. It hit and tangled in some trees.

"If we went down in a field," he said, "there would have been no chance for us."

Cordon scrambled out of his canopy to safety, but Brown's right-side window was jammed. He pulled out a knife and smashed the plexiglas on the left

side and lowered himself to the ground.

"We landed right in the middle of a bunker complex," Brown said. "We wanted to get out of there in a hurry because of that and because our birds that have been hit with missiles went up in flames on impact. I'm really surprised we didn't."

"Three things saved us, really — one of the other birds yelled 'Missile!', so I was ready for it; we landed in trees which cushioned the shock; and before every flight, I always lock my shoulder harness. Not all Cobra people do. If I hadn't, I'd have been thrown through the windshield."

Brown and Cordon ran into a clearing and waved their arms. Two other "Max" birds of the F Btry., 79th Arty., based at Long Thanh, swooped down to treetop level. One of the crewmen signalled Brown with a thumbs-up to indicate help was on the way. Ten minutes later, about 2:40 p.m., Brown said, a "Huey" chopper rescued the two Cobra fliers, along with several airborne troops.

Four other "Max" choppers have been destroyed — two of them by SA7s — and eight crewmen killed since April 7 when the unit began working the Loc Ninh-An Loc area.

Two of the men died Tuesday in the same area where Brown's chopper went down. They were hit by enemy ground fire, made a forced landing and were cut down by small arms fire as they ran from their aircraft.

APPENDIX V

(Remembrance by David Russell Toms written on January 20, 2011) :

MY REMEMBRANCES OF MISSILE!MISSILE!MISSILE!

Or

WHAT I REMEMBER ABOUT A MIRACULOUS DAY

My view as a participant:

On June 21, 1972, I believe it was in the early to mid afternoon, a heavy fire team of three Cobras (AH-1G) aircraft were assigned the task of escorting a flight of UH-1's on an insertion and extraction around a fire support base located on Highway 13. It was about half way between An Loc and Lai Khe, near the Hamlet of Chon Thanh. ARVN was making a push to retake An Loc from the south, if I remember correctly.

The three Cobra A/C's (aircraft commanders) were Ron Tusi, Mike Brown, and myself. Tusi was lead (I apologize deeply for not remembering all the front seat pilots; they were brave men all). The formation approached the landing zone from the east/southeast. Ron was flying low with the Slicks (UH-1's). Mike and I were flying escort cover from altitude. I was at 3,000' and Mike was at about 4,000'. As the flight was on short final Tusi yelled on the radio the infamous, "MISSILE, MISSILE, MISSILE." Quite a few things went through my mind in an extremely short period of time. One was "not again" (and that is another story). After about 2-3 seconds I figured that it was not going to hit me. I looked up at Mike's aircraft. He had been hit and the tail boom was falling away. It was very interesting how it separated. It was falling forward, down and to the left (aft looking forward). It was almost as though a saw had cut it off at the "4 Bolt" joint. No loose pieces, hanging wires, drives shaft, etc. Seeing this and fearful another missile might soon be on its way, I pushed the nose over, dropped the collective, and kicked the aircraft out of trim. We dropped like a rock. I recovered at the tree tops and I Looked to see Mike at about 1500-2000 feet. He was slowly coming down in a flat spin. My thoughts at the time were not hopeful. I circled the area that I presumed that he would come down in. Once he hit the trees, we went to find them thinking that this would be a recovery mission (I guess I could have been more optimistic, but it did not look good). Once we found the aircraft, we were surprised and elated. Mike was up and around and waving at us. Marco was also moving around. (As a side note, the aircraft was on its side—left I believe—and several trees were knocked down). Mike had crashed in a wooded area, which I believe was an aid to his survival. The trees kept him from spinning violently when he pulled collective at the bottom, thereby preventing any neck injuries.

I then asked my front seat pilot to lay out a few 40mm rounds (Again, I apologize profusely, can see the face, not the name. It pains me). He dutifully sent the rounds flying. The reason for this was that we knew that there had been NVA troops in the area and it was an attempt to ward them off. I then looked around to assess the situation as to how we might effect a rescue (much better than a recovery). I attempted to contact Ron Tusi but to no avail. The Slicks were getting ready to come out of the LZ, and I was extremely concerned about the welfare of Ron and his pilot (which I thought was Alan Russo, but he said that he doesn't think it was him—what is it that they say one loses first?). I then saw Tusi landing outside the wooded area. He had blown off his rocket pods, which would have been an essential action if he was to rescue Mike and Marco. He then got out of his aircraft along with his "front seat" and they started to run into the woods. I was at a bit of a loss as to what to do, with two crews on the ground. [23]

Seeing the Hueys coming out of the LZ. I called up their lead and

---

[23]This was not the first time Ron had done something like this. He was brave and fearless man and an ex- Navy corpsman and UDT Specialist (precursors of SEALS). Before we started this tour we were both at Cobra Instructor Pilot school. One evening in the "O" Club, I was sitting with a classmate of mine. He said to me, "You see that fellow over at the bar with the wavy hair?" I responded, "Yes, that's Tusi." The classmate then proceeded to tell me the following tale. He and Tusi were in the same unit on their last tour in RVN. One day Ron, as aircraft commander, was shot down. They arrived on scene to pick them up. The front seater was dead, and Ron was nowhere to be found. They looked for him for quite a while, but no joy. Approximately 2-3 weeks later he walked back into their base and headed straight to G2 (intelligence) and debriefed for approximately 2 days. It appears that he reverted to old habits? I was impressed.

asked for an aircraft to rescue Mike and Marco. After some discussion and coordination a Huey was flying to the crash area to determine if they could pick Mike and Marco (M&M) up. I was trying to position our aircraft so that I might be able to see Ron and company and the operation to get M&M out. I could not see or find Ron. I was talking the Huey down. He was skeptical that he could perform the operation safely, but try, he did! His crew chief and gunner were hanging out of the aircraft to help provide direction for clearance. The Huey was starting to take out a small tree with his tail rotor and had gotten as low as he could go. Mike then jumped up and the aircraft crew grabbed his arms and pulled him onboard. It was now Marco's turn. Marco is not a man of great physical stature where Mike was. In addition, we were not aware of the compression fractures that Marco had suffered during the crash. [24] He kept trying to jump up but they could not reach him. The Huey pilot skillfully and courageously lowered the aircraft more and more until they were finally able to effect Marco's recovery.

At this point my whole focus turned toward Ron. As I was looking for him and his "front seat," they were observed bounding out of the woods. I loitered on station until Ron took off. We then flew back to Lai Khe and met up with Mike. We talked a bit. Mike relayed some of his thoughts, etc. Ron had said the area he was running through was full of bunkers and fortified positions. I don't remember talking with Marco, because I believe that he was being medevacked out.

While this was just another view of the previously related incident (which may have some mental health value, but who knows?), there is one view that I have thought on for a long time after this incident. At the time of this incident I was very young and on my second tour as a Cobra pilot in Viet Nam. In my previous tour, I was in an Air Cav troop (same area of operations). As footnoted, I was shot down and crashed my first tour, all of which means little to nothing, except one

---

[24] I was told that Marco flew Slicks his first tour (I don't remember who told me this). At about the fourth month of that tour he was flying co-pilot on a "Hot insertion." As they were performing their flare, prior to landing, they received the "gift" of a B-40 rocket in the belly of their aircraft. The aircraft subsequently crashed and Marco suffered a compression fracture. This might explain the physical stature he had. (I lost almost three inches in height as the result of a compression fracture from being shot down on my first tour. I can empathize). Oh, by the way, this incident occurred at about his 4 month mark in this tour. Intersting.

thing. I have seen as many others have also, men wounded, some killed, and some you just knew were "dead," but suffered little to no harm. I believe that most, if not all helicopter pilots in RVN, have witnessed the same, as have other combatants. There were times that I thought I was going to die or be severely damaged. I have seen aircraft full of holes and the only bullet that came near the pilot was the one that went between his toes.

On the other hand I have seen one and only one bullet go through an aircraft. That bullet passed through a close friend's neck (and he drowned in his own blood). Now why the macabre thoughts as a part of this story? Well, it is not about macabre; it is about the hand of God. Some call them miracles, serendipity, being at the wrong place at the right time, etc. It may seem that events such as these are unexplainable. They are not. While we may witness these events more readily in a combat environment, we see them every day. We see it in the wonders and order of our world. I see it outside my window, when an oak grows out of granite rock, the rising sun, the teeming and ordered life all around us, and the finality of its physical end. I see the hand of God. Mike, Marco, myself, the Slick guys (and their passengers) and Ron, etc. all witnessed the hand of God. In this case it brings great joy. In other cases it is a time of sadness. In all cases, it reminds us of our humanity, our frailty, and God's sovereignty. Unfortunately/fortunately His hand is very obvious in combat. I am thankful for God's mercy on all of us (and our present and future families) on that day. None of us "deserved" His mercy on that day. It shall always be a wonder of wonders that the sun still rises each day. I hope that I will always be thankful and appreciative to Him and to those who share this life with me. Thank you for your patience as I reminisced and rambled.

APPENDIX VI

Selected Photos

Situation described on page 35—Blue Max maintenance crews rigging crashed Cobra in Lai Khe for CH-47 sling load to Bien Hoa. Several ARVN troops observing. Larry McKay standing in center with back to camera observes process.

Typical Blue Max escort mission—Troops loading in pickup zone while Blue Max Cobra at upper left provides gun cover.

Front Row (l-r): Billy Causey, Larry McKay, Barry McIntyre (kneeling). Back Row: Mike Brown (author), Steve Shields (KIA), John Henn (KIA), Steven Smith, Sam Hurt, unk, unk.

The last day of "Blue Max" F Battery 79th Aerial Field Artillery,
229th Assault Helicopter Battalion in Vietnam, August 1, 1972
Back Row(l to r) Garrett, Kedrow, Toms, Parker, Laguens, Tusi, Phillips, Robinson, Funk
Front row(l to r) Harmeling, Gower, Causey, Russo, Clausen, UNK, Baskett, Dobesh, Hurt

Mary and I with our earnest young guide, Truong, in front of former South Vietnam National Palace in December 1991 (See Chapter XVII—Return to Vietnam)

Saigon street activity viewed from balcony of our hotel, Return to VietnamDecember 1991

Furniture moving business, Saigon 1991
(Chapter XVII—Return to Vietnam)

Decapitated Statue at Catholic Church in An Loc
(See Chapter XVII—Return to Vietnam)

Made in the USA
San Bernardino, CA
26 November 2013